MW01001017

Commendations for *Gospel Conversations Reimagined*

"Cas Monaco has provided us with a very well written, captivating, full of narratives, and vitally important book. It is always easy to simply discredit our predecessors from our own position of 'enlightenment.' Cas does not make this mistake. She honors the remarkable legacy of Bill Bright by helpfully situating him in his context, and then leads the reader through a careful rethinking of personal evangelism along missional lines for today. In the process none of Cas's passion for evangelism or its importance is in any way diminished. If anything, it grows in importance even as it takes on a wonderfully more human shape. My hope is that this book will be widely read and discussed within Cru—a very significant organization—and far beyond. Cas's voice rings with contemporary authenticity and we need to attend to it."

—Craig Bartholomew, director, Kirby Laing Centre for Public Theology

"In our current context, when we attempt to share the good news of Jesus Christ, we often feel like a ship lost at sea. The choppy currents of cultural shifts and the stormy seas of secularization have shipwrecked many evangelistic endeavors. *Gospel Conversations Reimagined* is a lighthouse offering a beacon that illuminates theological, historical, and intensely practical insights that shine the light of hope that our words and witness can still lead those we love to the safe harbors of God's grace."

—Rasool Berry, director of partnerships and content development, Voices from Our Daily Bread Ministries

"We need to shift our approach to evangelism from making a bold presentation to engaging in a relational conversation. This is a central component of the argument that Cas Monaco makes in this important book regarding the necessity of 'recontextualizing' our approaches to evangelism in the 21st century. This book is critical and timely—many of our mid-to-late 20th century methodologies are no longer connecting with people like they once did. This book is biblical and theological—the recontextualized approach is carefully grounded within the Bible and God's mission. The results are personal and relevant. Numerous personal stories and examples are provided that make the challenge of a different approach we need to use today. A must read for anyone seeking to be a faithful and effective witness to the good news of the gospel in the world we now inhabit."

—Craig Van Gelder, emeritus professor of congregational mission, Luther Seminary

"Few would doubt that foundations of the evangelicalism that we have known to date are crumbling. There are many reasons for it, but I'm convinced that it is in part because we have never adjusted ourselves to the profoundly missional context we are now immersed in—like it or not. My friend Cas Monaco does a great job at helping us negotiate a way to a much more missionally faithful proclamation. This is an important read."

—Alan Hirsch, founder, Movement Leaders Collective

"With well-organized frameworks, Cas Monaco grapples with what it means to reimagine gospel presentations in fresh contexts. While weaving in her personal journey and scholarly research, she helps us think deeply about how we talk about Jesus and the kinds of conversations that help people move closer to him."

—Heather Holleman, associate teaching professor of advanced writing, Penn State

"Carefully researched, thoughtful, spiritually centered, and insightful, Cas Monaco's *Gospel Conversations Reimagined* is a must-read for anyone interested in sharing the good news in the world today. Dr. Monaco's passion for Jesus and for people is on clear display throughout the pages of this book, and her contextualized tools for sharing the gospel are thought-provoking and wise."

—Matt Mikalatos, author and speaker

"In today's argument culture we are fearful of having difficult conversations about social issues, politics, and especially religion. Many of us know we should speak up about Christ but can't imagine how. Cas Monaco helps us remember and reimagine the power, beauty, and primacy of evangelism. I've known her for over three decades and can't think of a better guide out of our evangelistic slumber."

—Tim Muehlhoff, professor of communication, Biola University

"The church tends to allow the innovative ministry models of one generation to become sacred cows of the next. We shout 'sacrilege' if anyone questions the need for revision in light of shifting cultural contexts. Part history lesson, part biblical and social research, and part personal journey, *Gospel Conversations Reimagined* reminds readers of the importance of God's mission, contextualization, and the art of listening and adapting in evangelism. With much experience, insight, and grace, Cas Monaco extends an exhortatory appeal for the church to discern how she equips members and engages the world with the gospel. Monaco wisely draws our attention to the fact those who have gone before had to build on the past and adjust to the challenges of their age—and we must do no less!"

—J. D. Payne, professor of Christian ministry, Samford University

"The spiritual landscape of our nation has changed significantly over the last few decades. The cultural context of our time looks very different than that of the mid-20th century, a time where many evangelistic approaches emerged within conservative evangelicalism. In *Gospel Conversation Reimagined*, Cas not only builds a compelling case for faithful recontextualization, she also delivers practical solutions in how we can engage in meaningful gospel conversations in our cultural moment. This work is a must read for the church as we navigate the present and growing shifts in culture."

—Niko Peele, founder and director, Ignite Movement

"Cas Monaco has a lifetime of experience communicating the good news of Jesus with those who are far from God. In this timely book, she draws not only from the well of experience, but more importantly from the deep mines of careful research at the intersection of theology and mission. The result is a timely road map for engaging in culturally informed and biblically faithful gospel conversations in the most winsome of ways. I'm convinced that if Dr. Bill Bright were still living on this side of eternity that he would enthusiastically commend her reimagined approach to personal evangelism. Why? Because his desire, like hers, was always to equip the redeemed to engage the lost in such a way that Jesus is made famous near and far. As you read through *Gospel Conversations Reimagined*, be prepared to find your part in God's amazing story of redemption precisely because you were not only saved from your sin by this gospel. You were saved onto mission with God!"

—George G. Robinson, professor of global disciple making and Bailey Smith Chair of Evangelism, Southeastern Baptist Theological Seminary

"This book peels back the curtain on why many of us feel confused, stuck, and fearful toward the evangelistic task in today's culture. Cas brings a deep level of clarity to the cultural shifts we are encountering, but likely do not fully understand. Cas also provides a thoughtful pathway towards re-engagement. Her admonition to take on the posture of a learner and intentionally move from presentation to conversation will bring a renewed sense of hope and confidence to participate in God's true story once again. This is a must read for every follower of Christ."

—Gary A. Runn, founder, Vocāre Leadership

"Dr. Cas Monaco has gifted a valuable resource to Cru and missionaries. In her book, she helps us to understand the importance of rethinking evangelism. She examines the religious context of the mid-20th century, yet Cas gives us more than a progress report. She introduces a new theological framework to connect with people through relationships. I do not know of a better book than this one for anyone looking to have more meaningful gospel conversations."

—Yamit Saliceti, professor of ethics and humanities, Hallmark University

"*Gospel Conversations Reimagined* is a must read to understand how to effectively communicate the gospel in today's secularized culture. Cas has done the research for us and has succinctly communicated how we can effectively engage people in conversation that is not weird or awkward! I personally love her stories that help us imagine what these conversations might look like."

—Pam Strain, director of LIFT Movement

"Cas Monaco's *Gospel Conversations Reimagined* is a thought-provoking exploration of the changing landscape of evangelism. As one committed to personal evangelism

Cas adeptly explores how traditional evangelistic tools and methodologies that once resonated with young people have lost their effectiveness. Her call to reimagine fresh, relevant methods for engaging in gospel conversations provides the new wineskins where God can do something new. A timely and inspiring must-read for those seeking to make the timeless message of the gospel resonate with people today."

—*Eric Swanson, senior fellow, Leadership Network*

"Cas's *Gospel Conversations Reimagined* is an important and practical resource in learning to engage our post-Christian world today. She provides a solid missiological and theological framework in re-contextualizing the gospel for effective evangelism today. I highly recommend her book to anyone seeking to be an effective disciple and witness of Jesus in our cities and culture today."

—*Faye Nakamura Waidley, executive director of oneness and diversity, Cru International*

"Cas Monaco is a voice for the mission of God in North America in our day. She has delved deeply into one of the most impactful evangelistic movements of the last century and carefully extracted the context, leadership, and innovation that gave birth to it. But more than that, she has revealed how these learnings need to be applied in our day and how evangelism must be reimagined in our context. Through the lens of more than forty years of frontline evangelistic experience, her thorough research and Spirit-led insight is a gift for all of us who desperately long for people to know Jesus. *Gospel Conversations Reimagined* is *the* conversation of our moment."

—*Darren Young, president, Power2Change*

Commendations for Hobbs College Library

"This series honors a wonderful servant of Christ with a stellar lineup of contributors. What a gift to the body of Christ! My hope and prayer is that it will be widely read and used for the glory of God and the good of his Church."

—*Daniel L. Akin, president, Southeastern Baptist Theological Seminary*

"This series is a must-have, go-to resource for everyone who is serious about Bible study, teaching, and preaching. The authors are committed to the authority of the Bible and the vitality of the local church. I am excited about the kingdom impact of this much-needed resource."

—*Hance Dilbeck, executive director, Baptist General Convention of Oklahoma*

"This series offers an outstanding opportunity for leaders of all kinds to strengthen their knowledge of God, his word, and the manner in which we should engage the culture around us. Do not miss this opportunity to grow as a disciple of Jesus and as a leader of his church."

—*Micah Fries, senior pastor, Brainerd Baptist Church, Chattanooga, TN*

"The best resources are those that develop the church theologically while instructing her practically in the work of the Great Commission. Dr. Thomas has assembled an impressive host of contributors for a new set of resources that will equip leaders at all levels who want to leave a lasting impact for the gospel. Dr. Hobbs exemplified the pastor-leader-theologian, and it's inspiring to see a series put out in his name that so aptly embodies his ministry and calling."

—*J.D. Greear, pastor, The Summit Church, Raleigh-Durham, NC, and former president, the Southern Baptist Convention*

GOSPEL CONVERSATIONS REIMAGINED

GOSPEL CONVERSATIONS REIMAGINED

A Missional Framework for Today

CAS MONACO

HEATH A. THOMAS, *Editor*

OBU

ACADEMIC

BRENTWOOD, TENNESSEE

Gospel Conversations Reimagined: A Missional Framework for Today
Copyright © 2024 by Cas Monaco

Published by B&H Academic
Brentwood, Tennessee
All rights reserved.

ISBN: 978-1-0877-7604-0

Dewey Decimal Classification: 269.2
Subject Heading: EVANGELISTIC WORK \ GOSPEL \ MISSIONS

Printed in the United States of America
29 28 27 26 25 24 VP 1 2 3 4 5 6 7 8 9 10

Dedication

To Bob

I love you and love following The Thread with you.
Thank you for reimagining gospel conversations
with me over countless discussions
and even more cups of coffee.

Contents

Acknowledgments   xv

About the Library   xvii

1. Recontextualizing Evangelism for a Twenty-First-Century
   Context   1

2. A Reality Check   23

3. Finding Our Bearings in the True Story of the Whole
   World   41

4. From Presentation to Conversation   61

5. Introducing a Missional Framework   77

6. Cultivating Faithful Recontextualization   93

   Recommended Reading   119

   Bibliography   125

   Name and Subject Index   131

   Scripture Index   137

Acknowledgments

I owe a debt of gratitude to Heath Thomas, who catalyzed my love of learning and urged me to become a scholar. Thank you for inviting me to contribute to this series.

I am deeply grateful to Craig Van Gelder for his willingness to read the various drafts of this book and for his excellent feedback. Craig, through his example and scholarship, has taught me what it means to be a theologian and a missiologist.

About the Library

The Hobbs College Library equips Christians with tools for growing in the faith and for effective ministry. The library trains its readers in three major areas: Bible, theology, and ministry. The series originates from the Herschel H. Hobbs College of Theology and Ministry at Oklahoma Baptist University, where biblical, orthodox, and practical education lies at its core. Training the next generation was important for the great Baptist statesman Dr. Herschel H. Hobbs, and the Hobbs College that bears his name fosters that same vision.

The Hobbs College Library: Biblical. Orthodox. Practical.

CHAPTER 1

Recontextualizing Evangelism for a Twenty-First-Century Context

In 2022, I celebrated my fortieth year of full-time ministry. I had placed my faith in Christ between my freshman and sophomore year of college. Soon after, I joined Campus Crusade for Christ (CCC, now Cru) at the University of Utah, where I received training on how to present the gospel using *Four Spiritual Laws*, a simple, four-point outline that explains the message of salvation. *Four Spiritual Laws*, developed by CCC founder, Bill Bright (1921–2003), and published in 1964, has been translated into innumerable languages and distributed to billions of people worldwide. I have always loved to share my faith and often carried a stack of *Four Spiritual Laws* with me wherever I went, and I was confident in my approach—that is, until a few years ago, when I met a college freshman at Portland State University (PSU).

Twenty-First-Century Shifts

On a fall afternoon, a PSU student and I decided to see if we could find someone who would be willing to answer some questions on our religious survey. I had taken hundreds of surveys like this one over the years and looked forward to finding someone with whom to speak. We approached a student in the cafeteria who was willing to take our survey. She was attending college in the heart of down-town Portland, but she grew up on a farm in central Oregon. We asked her the first question on the survey, "Who, in your opinion, is Jesus Christ?" Her whole demeanor immediately changed. Suddenly confused and bewildered, she replied, "I have no idea what you are talking about."

Furthermore, her answers to the rest of the survey questions indicated that she knew nothing about God or the Bible. I recall thinking, "How is it possible that a quintessential farm girl raised in America has never heard of Jesus?" Her faltering answers to Cru's standard religious survey rattled the foundation of my confidence, especially as I continued to encounter people who hesitated or declined to talk about God. This type of response threw me off balance and tempted me to either stop taking the initiative or stop sharing the gospel altogether.

Instead, God slowly turned my confusion into curiosity, and I began to do some research to better understand more about *Four Spiritual Laws*, the evangelistic tract I had used for over three decades. I knew that Bill Bright led the charge in promoting personal evangelism and personal evangelism training in the mid-twentieth century, but I never considered what exactly compelled him to write the tract. I ended up devoting my master's and PhD studies to researching this phenomenon to better understand Bright's mid-century context and to consider relevant ways to engage in what I now describe as "meaningful gospel conversations."[1]

God began bringing people into my life who shared my confusion and disorientation. We banded together and formed an

---

[1] Cas Monaco, "Bill Bright's (1921–2003) *Four Spiritual Laws* Reimagined: A Narrative Approach to Meaningful Gospel Conversations for an American Twenty-First-Century Secularized Context." PhD diss., Southeastern Baptist Theological Seminary, 2020, xv.

"Evangelism Think Tank" to help us learn in community. Among other things, we discovered that today's context stands in sharp contrast to America's mid-twentieth-century context from which emerged most of the evangelism methodologies still used by many evangelicals today, including *Four Spiritual Laws.*

When I joined the CCC staff in 1982, Bill Bright was at the helm. He often told us about his childhood in Coweta, Oklahoma, and frequently reminisced about his move to Hollywood, California, and subsequent conversion. He referred to Henrietta Mears, her consequent impact on his life, and her influence related to the founding of CCC. He never tired of casting vision for the fulfillment of the Great Commission and the significance of *Four Spiritual Laws.* It was easy to feel like I knew the story already, but to answer my question, "Why *Four Spiritual Laws?*" I would have to probe more deeply.

In the following sections I provide a brief synopsis of my findings. First, I provide a summary of Bright's life, including his upbringing and conversion. Second, I consider certain factors that lend insight into Bright's context from the vantage point of theology, history, and sociology. I also provide a summary of Henrietta Mears's influence in Bright's life and her impact on mid-twentieth-century evangelicalism. Third, I demonstrate the impact of these influences on Bright's vision for CCC, his strategy for fulfilling the Great Commission, and the force of this strategy that impacted his, and our, approach to evangelism. Fourth, I introduce a variety of ways he practiced contextualization through innovation. I wrap up this chapter by proposing that, just as Bright practiced contextualization in the mid-twentieth century, we need to do the same in the twenty-first century.

Understanding Bill Bright's Context

Bright's Upbringing

William R. Bright (1921–2003), born and raised on the cusp of the Great Depression, grew up on a ranch near Coweta, Oklahoma, in a home with no running water or electricity. Bright's character and work ethic, shaped by his saintly mother's prayers and honed by his hard-driving father, fueled his leadership and lifelong entrepreneurial determination.

Bill's grandfather, Samuel Bright, who benefited financially from the Oklahoma oil boom (1901–1905), purchased thousands of acres of land for his sons, including the 5,000-acre ranch where Bright was raised. Michael Richardson notes, "Samuel Bright . . . was one of the brave souls who . . . saddled up for the great land-grant rushes between 1889 and 1895 that had so transformed the Indian Territory." [2] Bill's father, Forrest Dale Bright, and grandfather both modeled a commitment to public service and politics by their active involvement in the Republican Party of Waggoner County, Oklahoma. When the Brights hosted evening events for gubernatorial and congressional candidates, Bill regularly presided as Master of Ceremonies.

Bright graduated with honors from Northeastern State University in Tahlequah, Oklahoma, in 1944. In that same year, three years after the bombing of Pearl Harbor, Bill enlisted in the army, but was disqualified due to a lingering football injury. Undeterred, he headed to Hollywood to enlist a second time, hoping the military might overlook his injury, but again to no avail.

---

[2]   Michael Richardson, *Amazing Faith: The Authorized Biography of Bill Bright* (Colorado Springs: WaterBrook, 2000), 292.

Bright's Conversion

After the disappointment of being turned down by the military again, Bright decided to start his own business, "Bright's California Confections."[3] During this time, he described himself as an agnostic, "not knowing whether God existed and not really caring if He did."[4] With the so-called good life as his goal, he believed, like his father and grandfather before him, that "a man can do anything he wants to do, on his own."[5] Providentially, on his first night in Los Angeles Bright picked up a hitchhiker who happened to be the founder of The Navigators, Dawson Trotman. He encouraged Bill to join him at a birthday celebration honoring his friend Daniel Fuller. In the years to come, both Daniel and his father, Charles E. Fuller, the founder of Fuller Seminary, would play an important role in Bill's life and ministry.

Bright's California landlords attended First Presbyterian Church of Hollywood (FPCH) and frequently invited him to attend church. Now and then, he recalled, he would show up on a Sunday morning and sit in the back row, until one day he agreed to attend a party sponsored by the FPCH College Department. He remembers being surprised by the turnout. The people there were unexpectedly friendly and outgoing, materially wealthy, and successful, but, even more unexpected, they loved Jesus Christ and claimed that nothing compared to knowing him.

Before long, Bright began attending FPCH's college class and met Henrietta Mears (1890–1963), FPCH's Director of Christian Education and the College Department. One Sunday in 1945, Mears described Paul's conversion on the road to Damascus and

---

[3]   Richardson, 18.

[4]   Bill Bright, *Come Help Change the World* (Peachtree, GA: Bright Media Foundation and Campus Crusade for Christ, 1999), loc. 197, Kindle.

[5]   Bright, loc. 187.

challenged her audience to consider this question: "Who are you, Lord, and what will you have me to do?" Bright, later that evening, knelt before God and prayed. "[I] asked the question with which Dr. Mears had challenged us.... Through my study I now believed that Jesus Christ was the Son of God, that he died for my sin, and that, as Dr. Mears had shared with us, if I invited him into my life as Savior and Lord, he would come in."[6] Soon Mears recognized Bright's zeal and natural leadership style and appointed him Sunday school president. Within a few short years, Vonette Zachary (1926–2015), Bright's skeptical fiancée, experienced conversion after hearing Mears's rational explanation of the gospel. Bill and Vonette were married in 1948.

Historical, Theological, and Sociological Influences

My research also led me to consider the historical foundations of Bill Bright's theology, which, as I discovered, traced back to the seventeenth-century Great Awakenings and revivalism. In the seventeenth century, revivalism came to be characterized by crisis conversion, sacrifice, and surrender. By the late seventeenth and early eighteenth century, revivalism included a heightened commitment to evangelism and foreign missions, especially among Protestants.

In 1792, William Carey, a Particular Baptist pastor and long-time missionary to India, came to prominence through his seminal document, "An Enquiry into the Obligation of Christians to Use Means for the Conversion of the Heathens."[7] In it, Carey argues that the Great Commission (Matt 28:18–20), a binding call for every Christian, provided the impetus for the spread of the gospel. Up until the eighteenth

---

[6] Bright, loc. 237.

[7] William Carey, *An Enquiry into the Obligation of Christians to Use Means for the Conversion of the Heathens* (London: The Carey Kingsgate Press Limited, 1792).

century, it was generally held that the Great Commission had applied only to the apostles, but Carey contends that every Christian is obligated to help fulfill the Great Commission. Subsequently, Carey, often described by Protestants as the Father of Modern Missions,[8] developed freestanding mission societies and systems for volunteerism. These systems propelled foreign missions into a new era described by missiologists as The Great Century of Missions.[9]

By the late nineteenth century, a "premillennial urgency" subordinated evangelistic concern to crisis conversion, soul saving, and practical Christianity.[10] D. L. Moody, a revivalist and significant contributor to the emerging fundamentalist movement, also emphasized the fulfilling of the Great Commission.[11] His vision included church cooperation among different denominations and connecting revivalism to social reform, evidenced in part by his efforts to

---

[8]   William Carey's contribution to the modern missions movement and his interpretation of the Great Commission have greatly impacted missions. David J. Bosch describes Carey as one of the many figures from that period who set out to "[Propagate] the Gospel Among the Heathen; . . . he was . . . as much a product as a shaper of the spirit of the time." *Transforming Mission: Paradigm Shifts in Theology of Mission*, American Society of Missiology Series, no. 16 (Maryknoll, NY: Orbis, 1991, 2011), 286. Craig Van Gelder and Dwight J. Zscheile describe Carey as one among many figures to contribute to the missions movement. *Participating in God's Mission: A Theological Missiology for the Church in America* (Grand Rapids: Eerdmans, 2018), 113.

[9]   Kenneth Scott Latourette, *A History of the Expansion of Christianity*, vol. 6 (New York: Harper and Row, 1937), 443. Notably, Paul E. Pierson, in "Colonialism and Missions," *EDWM* 209, adds that this era was rooted in eighteenth- and nineteenth-century revivalism and emphasized both evangelism and vigorous humanitarianism.

[10]   Joel A. Carpenter, *Revive Us Again: The Reawakening of American Fundamentalism* (New York: Oxford University Press, 1997), 248.

[11]   C. T. McIntire, in "Fundamentalism," *EDT* 472, defines fundamentalism as: "A movement that arose in the United States during and immediately after World War I to reaffirm orthodox Protestant Christianity and defend against liberal theology, German higher criticism, Darwinism, and other ideologies regarded as harmful."

care for poverty-stricken children. Importantly, his commitment to evangelism catalyzed the Student Volunteer Movement (under the leadership of John R. Mott) and rallied around "the evangelization of the world in this generation."[12] Bosch observes, "As revivalism and evangelicalism slowly adopted premillennialism, the emphasis shifted away from social involvement to exclusively verbal evangelism."[13]

Moody's premillennial urgency is illustrated by his watchword, "I look upon this world as a wrecked vessel. God has given me a lifeboat and said to me, 'Moody, save all you can.'"[14] The ravages of WWI in the early twentieth century and the devastation wrought by WWII in the mid-twentieth century served to accentuate this urgency.

As I noted earlier, Bright placed his faith in Christ in 1945, the same year WWII came to an end. The US and global contexts at the time included the horrors of the Holocaust, the use of the atomic bomb on Hiroshima and Nagasaki, and the ensuing Cold War with Russia. An estimated 70–85 million people, roughly 3 percent of the world population in 1940, lost their lives because of WWII. In an American context, the end of the war included the end of Japanese American internment and the rise of the civil rights movement. The civil rights movement, then just beginning, challenged the Jim Crow laws that firmly reinforced the strict segregation then in place. Significant for Bright, the postwar context also brought with it the palpable threat of communism.

The population in the United States at the time of the 1940 census was just under 90 percent white and 10 percent African

---

[12]   John R. Mott, *The Evangelization of the World in This Generation* (New York: Student Volunteer Movement, 1901), 1.

[13]   Bosch, *Transforming Mission*, 325.

[14]   Timothy K. Beougher, "Moody, Dwight Lyman," *EDWM* 657.

American. In 1951, according to Gallup, 66 percent of America's population identified as Protestant, 24 percent as Catholic, and 4 percent as Jewish.[15] Of note, most of the evangelism tools and training conservative evangelicals are familiar with today emerged in this predominantly white, Protestant religious context.[16]

With this post-WWII American context in mind, we turn back to a Sunday school training conference, held at Forest Home Conference Center in 1947. Henrietta Mears, having just returned to California after traveling across war-torn Europe, described her firsthand witness of the catastrophic damage resulting from the fight against Hitler's Naziism. She sounded a sober and urgent call for evangelism: "During the war, men of special courage were called upon for difficult assignments; often these volunteers did not return. They were called 'expendables.' We must be [men and women of total commitment] expendables for Christ . . . [and] if we fail God's call tonight, we will be held responsible."[17] Bill Bright, Louis Evans Jr., and Richard Halverson responded to Mears's call that night, and

---

[15] Gallup, "Religion: Survey of American's population from 1948–2014," https://news.gallup.com/poll/1690/religion.aspx, n.p. This survey records responses to various questions, including the following: "What is your religious preference—are you Protestant, Roman Catholic, Mormon, Jewish, Muslim, another religion, or no religion?"

[16] Notable tools and approaches to evangelism developed in the mid-twentieth century by evangelicals include: (1) Dawson Trotman's (Founder of The Navigators) "Bridge to Life" in 1933 and subsequent discipleship materials that focused on helping new believers understand their conversion decision, https://www.navigators.org/about/history/; (2) The Billy Graham Evangelistic Association developed products and approaches to evangelism in the 1940s and 1950s that provided teaching and training following his revivals and radio program, *Hour of Decision*, https://billygraham.org/news/media-resources/electronic-press-kit/bgea-history/history/; (3) James Kennedy's "Evangelism Explosion" and the five "Kennedy questions," developed in 1962, also provided a specific approach to evangelism: https://evangelismexplosion.org/50-years-2-questions-millions-brought-to-jesus-part-1/.

[17] Richardson, *Amazing Faith*, 37.

in the shadow of WWII, they fanned the flames of the "Mid-Century Revival."[18] Before we examine the extent to which this revival impacted Bright's trajectory, let me provide, first, an overview of Henrietta Mears's background and theology.

Henrietta Mears

The more I studied Bright's mid-twentieth-century context, the more I realized the scope of Henrietta Mears's impact on his life. In fact, the foundation for Bright's ministry philosophy, and the evangelism tool *Four Spiritual Laws,* rested on her evangelical theology and revivalist influences. Notably, Mears's influential reach extended from FPCH to various prominent evangelical institutions including Princeton University, Fuller Seminary, and the National Association of Evangelicals. Her teaching and training curriculum reflected her evangelical and Protestant traditions, her commitment to the inerrancy of Scripture, and expository teaching. Mears emphasized spiritual regeneration, repentance from sin, and faith in Jesus Christ. She encouraged every believer to actively share the gospel, to engage in world missions, and to help to fulfill the Great Commission. Significantly, Wesleyan Holiness Theology and the Keswick Convention

---

[18] J. Edwin Orr, *The Second Evangelical Awakening in America* (London: Marshall, Morgan, and Scott, 1952). Scholars hold various points of view on the veracity of the Great Awakenings. These references are included for more information. Joe Butler, "Enthusiasm Described and Decried: The Great Awakening as Interpretive Fiction," *JAH* 69, no. 2 (1982); Thomas Kidd, in *The Great Awakening: The Roots of Evangelical Christianity in Colonial America* (New Haven: Yale University Press, 2009), argues for one continuous awakening between the 1730s and 1780s. J. Edwin Orr, *The Flaming Tongue: The Impact of Twentieth Century Revivals* (Chicago: Moody, 1973); "Hidden Springs," Lecture, 1963, location and exact date unknown, Campus Crusade for Christ Archives, Orlando, FL, contends for a mid-twentieth-century awakening with painstaking attention to detail. Orr played an influential role in Bright's life and in CCC, and I follow Orr's timeline.

held prominence in Mears's teaching and ministry philosophy, as demonstrated by her focus on the "higher life," absolute surrender, and the indwelling of and dependence on the Holy Spirit.[19]

Mears inherited her intense devotion, active participation in evangelism, and commitment to helping fulfill the Great Commission from her mother and maternal grandparents. Her mother, a devout woman of prayer and Bible study, modeled personal evangelism and taught Henrietta, by example, to take advantage of every opportunity to share the gospel. Henrietta also demonstrated aptitude for Bible teaching and taught her first Sunday school class at the age of eleven. Later, she founded the Willing Workers to care for people in need.[20]

Mears, a chemistry major at the University of Minnesota, continued to teach Bible classes, engage in evangelism, and encourage students to take the gospel to the world. Following graduation, she served under William B. Riley (1861–1947), who pastored First Baptist Church of Minneapolis, Minnesota, for forty years. Riley, an evangelist and reputed architect of fundamentalism, provided the basis for Mears's theological foundation.[21] Riley, founder of Northwestern Bible and Missionary Training School, afforded Mears ample opportunities to teach the Bible and train others. During this same time, Mears taught a Sunday school class for teenage girls and developed a model for evangelism and discipleship that resulted in unparalleled spiritual multiplication. Within a decade, over 3,000

---

[19]   Gary B. McGee, "Evangelical Movement," *EDWM* 337.

[20]   Andrea V. B. Madden, "Henrietta C. Mears 1890–1963," (master's thesis, Gordon-Conwell Theological Seminary, 1997), 11. The "The Willing Workers" cared for and served women in unfortunate and often destitute circumstances.

[21]   Barbara Hudson Powers, *The Henrietta Mears Story* (Westwood, NJ: Fleming H. Revell, 1957), 113.

young women received training in evangelism and discipleship under her tutelage.[22]

Mears's teaching and training early in her career paved the way for her long-term role as the Director of Christian Education for First Presbyterian Church of Hollywood from 1928 until 1963. There, she created a system of discipleship and a rigorous training program in evangelism for the College Department. In the 1930s, she founded Gospel Light Press where she published "age-graded" Sunday school curriculum—especially popular among fundamentalists at the time.[23]

Bright's Vision, the Great Commission, and *Four Spiritual Laws*

Bright followed Mears's lead and eventually patterned his approach to evangelism and discipleship after hers. He published curricula, including *Four Spiritual Laws*, with the goal of spreading the gospel through multiplication. Richardson's description of Bright is apropos: "Bill became a spark plug in the Mears ministry machine.... When it came to forging ahead with ways of pressing the message of Christ, Bill would try almost anything."[24]

Bright's Vision from God
In 1951, spurred by the events at Forest Home in 1947, Bright received a vision from God for the founding of CCC. Bright, with emotion, often retold his story of experiencing God's presence in tangible ways:

---

[22] Madden, "Henrietta C. Mears," 28.

[23] Madden, 44.

[24] Richardson, *Amazing Faith*, 27.

There was no audible voice; no heavenly choirs; no bright lights or bolts of lightning. However, the presence of the Almighty seemed so real that all I could do was wait expectantly for what He had to say. Within minutes I felt an amazing combination of peace and excitement, for I had the overwhelming impression that God had flashed on the screen of my mind His instructions for my life and ministry.[25]

God called him, definitively, to devote his entire life to the fulfillment of the Great Commission. "I was to begin by helping to win and disciple college students for Christ, since they are the leaders and influencers of tomorrow."[26] Bright shared this experience and vision with Dr. Wilbur Smith, Fuller Seminary professor. Smith, compelled by the potential of this opportunity, even suggested "CCC, Campus Crusade for Christ" as an appropriate name for this endeavor.[27] Smith went on to endorse Bright's calling:

From the time that the Lord laid upon his heart a great burden for a definite advance movement for evangelism on the campuses of our colleges and universities, Mr. William R. Bright has honored me by coming into my office to discuss ways and means, and personnel, for such a campaign as he visions…. My own opinion is that the Campus Crusade for Christ has the possibility, under the blessing of God, of being a milestone in the notable his-

---

25   Bill Bright, *Come Help*, loc. 370.
26   Bright, loc. 375.
27   Bright, loc. 386.

tory of work among college students in our beloved land.
Mr. Bright is worthy of all confidence.[28]

Bill Bright left seminary behind and started CCC at UCLA in 1951.
He was thirty years old.

Bright's Strategy to Help Fulfill the Great Commission

In 1945, World War II came to an end after the Allied forces declared
victory over Germany and Italy, and eventually Japan. This era also
marked the beginning of the Cold War between the United States
and the Union of Soviet Socialist Republics.[29] In 1966, Bright gave
a lecture at CCC's Dallas Lay Institute of Evangelism, titled, "A
Strategy for Fulfilling the Great Commission."[30] In it he shows keen
awareness of his context, evidenced by his resolve to defeat communist atheism, and he laments the prominence of spiritual and moral
corruption: "[We're] living in a desperate hour—not only internally
but without the threat of communism greater than ever [sic].… The
communists are determined to take the world and they are taking the
world."[31] He anticipated an all-encompassing move of God: "Instead
of communism taking the world, I'm personally persuaded that we
are going to see the fulfillment of the Great Commission."[32]

In his presentation he emphasized: (1) the significance of the
Great Commission—"It's a command of Christ, men are lost without

---

[28] Wilbur Smith, Letter of Endorsement, June 22, 1951, Campus Crusade for
Christ Archives, Orlando, FL.

[29] Van Gelder and Zscheile, *Participating in God's Mission*, 157.

[30] Bill Bright, "A Strategy for Fulfilling the Great Commission," Dallas Lay
Institute of Evangelism, February 13–20, 1966, Campus Crusade for Christ Archives,
Orlando, FL.

[31] Bright, 2.

[32] Bright, 3.

Christ, and men everywhere are hungry for God;"[33] and (2) the need for a strategy—"If we have a strategy this world can be reached in this generation and instead of the communist horde sweeping over the world, the Gospel of Jesus Christ…can go to the world."[34]

Later that same year, Bright presented a paper at the World Congress on Evangelism in Berlin titled, "Methods and Philosophy of Personal Evangelism."[35] This paper evidenced his resolve and gave place for his comprehensive vision. He stated, "If the Great Commission is to be fulfilled in our generation, there must be a dramatic new emphasis on personal evangelism."[36] He argued that the solution to feeble and cowardly evangelism must include vigorous training in the Spirit-filled life and personal evangelism for all Christian leaders and pastors.

The basis of his argument rested on the results of a survey he conducted that garnered thousands of responses. According to Bright, the survey indicated several reasons behind the absence of personal evangelism: (1) fear, busyness, and lack of training; (2) lack of fruitfulness due to carnality: "Approximately ninety-five percent of all Christians are living defeated, fruitless, carnal lives";[37] (3) lack of expertise and courage; (4) lack of belief: "The Christian has been brainwashed into presupposing a negative response to a personal witness for Christ."[38] He concludes with this declaration: "The Great Commission can and by God's grace shall be fulfilled

---

[33]   Bright, 4.

[34]   Bright, 4.

[35]   Bill Bright, "Methods and Philosophy of Personal Evangelism," presented at the World Congress on Evangelism, Kongresshalle, Berlin, October 26–November 4, 1966, Campus Crusade for Christ Archives, Orlando, FL.

[36]   Bright.

[37]   Bright.

[38]   Bright.

only through a renewed emphasis on personal evangelism."[39] Bright exhorts Christians to abide in Christ, appropriate the Spirit's power, prioritize personal evangelism, and receive training in how to share the gospel.

Four Spiritual Laws

As noted earlier, in 1951 more than 50 percent of America's population identified as Protestant, verifying research sponsored by CCC's *Collegiate Challenge* Magazine in 1964. In an article, "The Most Important Question Ever Asked: Answer Unknown by 89.1%," a reported 10,500 college students were interviewed on campuses across 17 states over a three year period. Although 92.1% indicated that they knew more about Jesus than any other religious leader and 62.7% believed Jesus to be the Son of God, a startling 89.1% did not know how to become Christians.[40] This one detail, perhaps more than any other, compelled Bright to develop *Four Spiritual Laws*.[41]

Bright firmly believed that leaders around the world were "waiting to hear the good news of God's love and purpose for their lives."[42] He admonished, "Most of the people with whom you speak are interested,"[43] and he vigorously maintained that the problem in evangelism rested on Christians who lacked training, commitment, and courage.[44] Nonetheless, particularly in the early 1960s,

---

[39] Bright.

[40] The Most Important Question Ever Asked: Answer Unknown by 89.1%," *The Collegiate Challenge Magazine*, 1, (May 1964), 11. Campus Crusade for Christ Archives, Orlando, FL.

[41] Richardson, *Amazing Faith*, 80.

[42] Bill Bright, "Student Power, The Campus Ministry of Campus Crusade for Christ," *Action Magazine: A Special Report* 1, no. 1 (Spring 1969): 8.

[43] Bright, "Strategy," 10.

[44] Bright, 7.

his emphasis on training in personal evangelism also reflected his concern for the unrest on college campuses. He states:

> During this time of unprecedented campus unrest and revolt, another revolution is taking place on the campuses of the world—a revolution of love, the total unconditional love of God. All around the world, the forces of materialism, secularism, atheism, and communism are battling for the minds of students. But students are seeking commitment to a cause big enough to demand their all, and the cause of Jesus Christ is proving to be just that big.... Staff members are serving on strategic campuses all across the nation.... It is their privilege daily to introduce students to Jesus Christ.[45]

In this context, Bill Bright developed *Four Spiritual Laws.* He took a risk at the time by introducing God's love first, before pointing out man's sin. This decision sparked criticism among conservative evangelicals and even some of his staff. But Bright held fast. God's love captivated him, and, from both a personal and theological standpoint, he concluded, "How could anyone say no to Christ if they truly understood how much He loves them? We needed to start with the positive!"[46] Soon, other churches and ministries like Billy Graham's Evangelistic Association followed his lead. At the same time, Bright also introduced various templates for sharing *Four Spiritual Laws,* like the Van Dusen Letter that specifically addressed wealthy businessmen.[47]

---

[45]   Bright, "Student Power," 8.

[46]   Bright, *Come Help*, loc. 647.

[47]   Bright, loc. 626–28. Bright wrote a personal letter to Howard Hughes, American business magnate, in 1947. He always led by example.

Bright's rigorous research provided the seedbed for his earliest strategies. The research revealed that most people surveyed indicated some familiarity with the first three Spiritual Laws: "God loves you and offers a wonderful plan for your life; Man is sinful and separated from God, therefore he cannot know and experience God's love and plan for his life; and Jesus Christ is God's only provision for man's sin."[48] In turn, the research also demonstrated a lack of awareness of God's love. In fact, this revelation shaped Law Four: "You must individually receive Jesus Christ as Savior and Lord, then you can know and experience God's love and plan for your life."[49] This point illustrated, through a simple diagram, a life separated from Christ on the one hand, and a life yielded to Jesus Christ on the other. It explained that by taking a simple step of faith, confessing sin, and receiving Christ's payment for sin, it was possible to know God personally and experience God's love. In 1957, the first prototype of *Four Spiritual Laws*, according to Bright, provided a clear and simple explanation for how individuals can know God personally. His critics often described it as "too simplistic."[50]

Evangelism and Innovation

Four Spiritual Laws, first formally published in 1964 in booklet form, has since been translated into countless languages and distributed to billions worldwide. Bill Bright, often described as an evangelical entrepreneur, went on to innovate a host of creative ways

---

[48]   Bill Bright, *Four Spiritual Laws* (Los Angeles: Campus Crusade for Christ, 1964).

[49]   Bright.

[50]   John G. Turner, *Bill Bright and Campus Crusade for Christ: The Renewal of Evangelicalism in Postwar America* (Chapel Hill: University of North Carolina Press, 2008), loc. 1305.

to communicate this simple message of God's love and plan and to answer the prevailing question in his context, "Is it true?" He provided a rational argument for the truth and historicity of Jesus in "The Uniqueness of Jesus," a multifaceted tool produced in the form of a small booklet and as a set of vinyl records.[51] This multi-album set served as the catalyst for utilizing cutting-edge technology in CCC's record ministry. Bright provided the impetus for *Jesus Film*, and he pressed the fundamentalist boundaries with *André Kole's World of Illusion*.

In 1964, Josh McDowell joined CCC to provide "well-documented historical, scientific, and biblical evidence for the Christian faith."[52] McDowell's apologetic skills, honed in discussions with Fascist and Marxist students in Latin America in the late 1960s, uniquely qualified him to interact with American university students in the 1970s.[53] McDowell's contributions include the apologetics series *Evidence that Demands A Verdict* and *The Resurrection Factor*.[54] McDowell's most widely distributed resource, *More Than A Carpenter*,[55] defends the claims of Christ—the purpose behind his death, burial, and resurrection—and provides evidence for the reliability of Scripture.

---

[51] Bill Bright, *A Handbook for Christian Maturity: Ten Basic Steps Toward Christian Maturity* (Orlando: New Life Publications, 1994).

[52] Bright, Come Help, loc. 1178.

[53] Josh McDowell, "My Story: Josh McDowell," Cru, My Story: How My Life Changed, https://www.cru.org/us/en/how-to-know-god/my-story-a-life-changed/my-story-josh-mcdowell.html

[54] Josh McDowell and Sean McDowell, *Evidence that Demands A Verdict* (Nashville: Thomas Nelson, 2017). Josh McDowell, *The Resurrection Factor* (Crownhill, Milton Keynes: Authentic Media, 2005).

[55] Josh McDowell, *More Than A Carpenter* (Wheaton: Tyndale, 2009).

Recontextualizing for a Twenty-First-Century Context

In the chapters that follow we will look closely at how the triune God sustains and promotes the gospel in imaginative and redemptive ways in all kinds of cultures and contexts. But the mere fact that we are discussing this topic over 2,000 years after Jesus's resurrection underscores this point. It reassures us that the gospel is strong and resilient and reinforces the fact that God makes contextualization possible.

This chapter demonstrated how Bill Bright practiced contextualization by learning, doing research, and paying attention to his predominantly white, Protestant, and post-WWII context. We noted in this chapter that his development of *Four Spiritual Laws* was born out of his desire to communicate the love of God and the message of salvation within this setting and in response to his research. The tools that emerged, including *Four Spiritual Laws,* reflected his use of cutting-edge technology and culturally relevant events and practices. So, it stands to reason that, since the US society and context has changed in dramatic ways, as was illustrated in my conversation with the student at Portland State, we must engage in faithful recontextualization of evangelism, just like Bill Bright did over seventy years ago.

Missiologist Paul Hiebert points out, "On the one hand, the gospel belongs to no culture. It is God's revelation of himself and his acts to all people. On the other hand, it must always be understood and expressed within human cultural forms."[56] Simply put, to contextualize or recontextualize means to proclaim the gospel amid all kinds of cultures. We must hold in tension the potential to over-contextualize by compromising or overadapting the gospel, and the

---

[56] Paul Hiebert, *Anthropological Insights for Missionaries* (Grand Rapids: Baker, 1985), 30.

possibility of undercontextualizing by resisting change in the name of tradition and biblical fidelity.

Reflection

Bill Bright's *Four Spiritual Laws,* an approach to evangelism designed in a context rife with disruption, provides us a ready example of contextualization. Bright's earliest presentations reveal a zealous effort to help fulfill the Great Commission by training people in personal evangelism. He purposed to provide an innovative, cutting-edge, and relatable tool to communicate this four-point message of salvation in ways that were both creative and attractive. Research reveals that he was especially moved by a desire to communicate God's love to Protestants who did not know or understand God's love and to quell the rising tide of communism. His purposes clearly reflect America's mid-twentieth-century context.

So, my initial research began to answer my first question, "Why *Four Spiritual Laws*?" but it raised many more. Eventually, I whittled down my questions to this one: "How can Cru train others to present the gospel in a twenty-first-century American context and honor Bill Bright's vision and maintain his commitment to evangelism?" As I took the next step and began investigating America's twenty-first-century context, my husband and I, on a flight from Raleigh-Durham, North Carolina to Portland, Oregon in 2018, had an engaging conversation with a fellow traveler. She had been raised as a Pentecostal and now identified as Wiccan, which resulted in a very different conversation from the ones I had with people coming from predominantly Protestant and Catholic backgrounds in the late 1970s and 1980s. This represents the perfect segue to chapter 2; A Reality Check.

A Reality Check

I flew into Chicago O'Hare on a Sunday afternoon in the fall of 2012 and hailed a cab for a quick ride to my hotel just a few miles away. The young driver barely spoke English, and he circled the airport twice before his GPS finally aimed us in the right direction. As we attempted a conversation, I could hear his Russian accent and soon learned that he hailed from Kazakhstan. I explained that I once lived in the former Soviet Union and had visited Kazakhstan a few times. He reacted with surprise and asked, "Why?" I responded with near perfect recall the one Russian phrase I will never forget, "We talked with university students about God."

Suddenly his demeanor changed as he simultaneously slowed way down and frantically fumbled around looking for his personal phone. I watched from the back seat as he nervously thumbed through YouTube videos and handed his phone back to me. The video playing on the screen displayed a Muslim imam debating with a priest about the virgin birth. The imam dominated. I sat in the back seat of that cab so curious, a bit stunned, and constrained to remain diligent in my research. This young Muslim Kazakh was sharing his faith with me in Chicago! We attempted a cordial, albeit halting, conversation about the viability of the virgin birth until we eventually arrived at the hotel. As we exited the car and met at the trunk, he handed me my bag, looked me in the eyes and said, "I believe it was Allah's will that we met today. I hope to see you in Paradise." I replied with equal conviction, "I believe it was the God of the Universe's will for us to meet today, and I hope to see you in heaven." As I pulled my bag into the hotel I wondered what in the world had just happened.

This experience, added to several others, confirmed my suspicions—America's context has changed, and is changing, in radical ways. My curiosity heightened and I pressed into my research with even greater purpose. I became increasingly convinced that now, more than ever, we need to understand the changes that are taking place in our context, especially if we purpose to engage in meaningful gospel conversations with our families, friends, neighbors, and coworkers.

In this chapter, I provide my findings from four missiological vantage points. From the first, I draw insight from Canadian philosopher Charles Taylor and explore the impact of secularization in an American context. From the second, I introduce "Understanding Faith and Purpose in the City,"[1] a research project conducted by Cru in 2016, which provides helpful insights related to gospel conversations. From the third, I highlight America's changing demographics due in large part to immigration and consider, in brief, the sociological and religious implications of these population changes in the United States. Finally, from the fourth vantage point, I introduce Gen Z (the generation born between 1999 and 2015) and some prevailing characteristics that contribute to their worldview.[2] These missiological snapshots provide insight into our secularized context, validate our experiences, and help us to reimagine meaningful gospel conversations.

---

[1]   Brooke Wright et al., "Understanding Faith and Purpose in the City" (Atlanta: Cyrano Marketing Collective, 2016).

[2]   See chapter 1: Recontextualizing Evangelism for a Twenty-First-Century Context.

Missiological Vantage Point 1: Introducing Secularization

As I demonstrated in chapter 1, *Four Spiritual Laws*, published in 1964, provides us with an excellent example of a "contextualized" approach to evangelism, based on research conducted on college campuses in the United States in the 1950s. Of the 10,500 students interviewed, most identified as Protestant, and very few knew about God's love or plan for their lives. Strikingly, although most identified as Protestants, very few knew about God's love or plan for their lives. As I noted in Chapter One, this revelation, above all others, motivated Bill Bright to develop *Four Spiritual Laws*. He remained adamant that leaders everywhere were "waiting to hear the good news of God's love and purpose for their lives,"[3] and insisted that Christians, fearful and untrained, lacked the commitment and courage to present the gospel. Bright's solution was straightforward— provide a simple tool and vigorous training in personal evangelism.

Although the tool's effectiveness at the time verifies Bright's assertion, I could not help but wonder, "Why, then, was it so appealing to believe in God in 1951, while in 2020 [and beyond] many find *not* believing in God easy and even preferable?"[4] My research led me to Canadian philosopher and culture critic, Charles Taylor, who lends insight into our current context. Here I draw from Taylor's definition of secularization and consequent exclusive humanism.

Charles Taylor's Secularization: What It Is and What It Is Not
Charles Taylor's tome, *A Secular Age*, helps us understand these cultural shifts by describing the process of *secularization*.[5] He describes our era as one in which people find belief in God implausible and

---

[3] Bright, "Student Power," 8 (see chap. 1, n. 42).

[4] Monaco, "Bill Bright's," 31 (see chap. 1, n.1).

[5] Charles Taylor, *A Secular Age* (Cambridge: Belknap, 2007), 500.

even unimaginable. Taylor posits that today people view the world based entirely on what they can explain or experience without any reference to God. But Taylor's secularism is not void of spirituality but is in fact a "super-nova—a kind of galloping pluralism on the spiritual plane."[6] In other words, Christianity is one belief option among an explosion of others.

Importantly, Taylor's secularization differs from a traditional evangelical understanding of *secular*. Since this term is used in a variety of ways, I provide a quick overview of the term. "The term 'secular' is derived from the Latin noun *saeculum* . . . signifying 'belonging to this age or the world' rather than to a transcendent religious order."[7] Moreover, some describe any activity not associated with religion as secular. *Secularism* is a view of the world that "finds little if any place for the supernatural and the transcendent" and separates government and religious institutions. Secularism passes off religious belief as implausible and powerless.[8] Unsurprisingly, both noun and adjective mark the absence of God and belief in God.

Secularization

Taylor provides a slightly different and insightful perspective regarding how to understand *secularization*. As mentioned above, Taylor's secular age is not void of belief, but instead is bursting with all kinds of beliefs.[9] Furthermore, in this secularized context, Christianity, no longer the predominant religion in America, competes with a vast array of other religions, philosophies, and spins on life. In other words, while many people in today's American context hold a set

---

[6] Taylor, 300.

[7] William H. Baker, "Secularist, Secularism," *EDWM* 865.

[8] Baker, 865.

[9] Taylor, *A Secular Age*, 300.

of beliefs, most consider belief in God far-fetched—even inconceivable. Taylor's secularization leads to the emergence of exclusive humanism. This is a democratic and ethical life stance claiming that morality is independent from theology and God, thereby affirming that humankind has a right and responsibility to shape their lives apart from God.

Sociologist Philip Rieff warns, "The . . . notion of a culture that persists independent of all sacred orders is unprecedented in human history."[10] He argues that this so-called liberation does not necessarily grant boundless permission, but instead, gives way to "endlessly contestable and infinitely changeable rules."[11] He takes this a step further and maintains that eliminating the sacred center inevitably leads from the inviolability of each unique human life to the negation of the human altogether.[12]

Missiological Vantage Point 2: Cru's Research

Chapter 1 introduced Bill Bright and the evangelistic tool he developed in his context: *Four Spiritual Laws*. As noted in Chapter One, we discovered his context to be religiously homogeneous, and one in which people more willingly listened to a presentation like *Four Spiritual Laws*.[13] However, as my Cru colleagues and I attempted to use *Four Spiritual Laws* in our current context, we encountered a

---

[10]   Philip Rieff, *My Life Among the Deathworks: Illustrations of the Aesthetics of Authority,* Vol. 1 of *Sacred Order/Social Order*, ed. Kenneth S. Piver (Charlottesville: University of Virginia Press, 2006), 13.

[11]   James Davison Hunter, introduction to *My Life Among the Deathworks: Illustrations of the Aesthetics of Authority*, by Philip Rieff (Charlottesville, VA: University of Virginia Press, 2006), xxii.

[12]   Rieff, *My Life*, 106.

[13]   Gallup, "Religion" (see chap. 1 n. 15).

new set of barriers. We found that people today do not understand familiar terms such as God, sin, guilt, or salvation, and often load these words with meanings we never intended.

Cru's Response to Cultural Shifts

Cru, a nondenominational evangelical organization, remains committed to helping fulfill the Great Commission. Like many parachurch organizations and denominations in the United States today, Cru seeks to remain attentive to today's cultural and sociological shifts and, overall, continues to engage in research and development to determine theologically sound and effective approaches to evangelism.

Campus Crusade for Christ Changes Name to Cru

As previously mentioned, Campus Crusade for Christ (CCC) began on the campus of UCLA in 1951, targeted student leaders, provided training in personal evangelism, and prioritized the presentation of *Four Spiritual Laws*. Bill and Vonette Bright, together with Henrietta Mears, began reaching students on the campus of one university. Today, CCC's scope includes a host of contextualized ministries and reaches a variety of audiences beyond the university campus.[14] *Christianity Today* reported in 2011, "The 60-year-old ministry is one of the largest evangelical parachurch organizations in the world, with about 25,000 staff members in 191 countries and $490 million in annual revenue."[15] The impact of CCC's outreach is undeniable.

---

[14] Monaco, "Bill Bright's," 129. These audiences include executives and professionals; families and athletes; artists and philanthropists; pastors in inner-city, urban, and suburban neighborhoods; and military personnel.

[15] Sarah Bailey, "Campus Crusade Changes Name to Cru," *Christianity Today*, July 19, 2011, http://www.christianitytoday.com/ct/2011/julyweb-only/campus-crusade-name-change.html.

CCC's US-based leadership, in certain ways, recognizes the tension between responding to the paradigmatic shifts in the culture and maintaining the founder's original vision. This included, after considerable research and prayerful collaboration, changing CCC's name to "Cru."[16] Steve Sellers, CCC International Vice President and US National Director at the time, explains, "[Crusade] has become a flash word for a lot of people. It harkens back to other periods of time and has a negative connotation for lots of people across the world, especially in the Middle East.... In the '50s, *crusade* was [an] evangelistic term in the United States. Over time, different words take on different meanings to different groups."[17]

Understanding Faith and Purpose in the City

Cru's name change served as the impetus for a focused effort to advance the mission of Jesus in key cities in the United States in 2011. Leaders sought to understand the current religious and cultural context in the United States to effectively engage in gospel conversations in a twenty-first-century urban context. Then, in 2016, Cru initiated a research project, "Understanding Faith and Purpose in the City."[18] The project included a careful assessment of the ministry's history, the philosophy behind Cru's approach to evangelism, and an inventory of resources developed over the years.

The project surveyed a group of 400 people living in major US cities. These men and women, ranging in ages between twenty-four and fifty-six, held different worldviews and represented a variety of ethnic backgrounds (see figure 1). Significantly, more than 50 percent claimed no religious affiliation and considered Christianity

---

[16] Cru is a familiar nickname adopted by students at the local level in the 1990s.

[17] Bailey, "Campus Crusade."

[18] Wright et al., "Understanding Faith."

"irrelevant, inauthentic, offensive, and even unsafe."[19] After analyzing the data, one of the members of the marketing firm remarked, "Christianity has a branding problem." We pressed on.

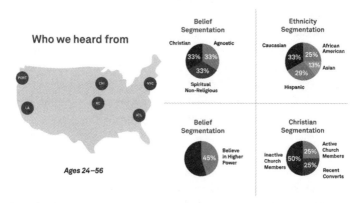

Figure 1. Infographic of Population Surveyed. Brooke Wright et al., "Understanding Faith and Purpose in the City," Atlanta: Cyrano Marketing Collective, 2016. Copyright Cru, 2018. Reprinted with permission.[20]

Personas and the Scale of Belief
Seven different personas emerged from the data (see figure 2) and represent six postures of belief.[21] Important to the findings, the italicized words used in each description below come directly from the respondents.

---

19   Monaco, "Bill Bright's," 130.
20   Wright et al., "Understanding Faith."
21   Wright et al.

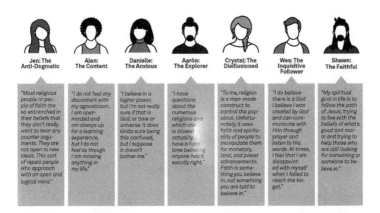

Jen: The Anti-Dogmatic	Alan: The Content	Danielle: The Anxious	Aarón: The Explorer	Crystal: The Disillusioned	Wes: The Inquisitive Follower	Shawn: The Faithful
"Most religious people or people of faith are so entrenched in their beliefs that they don't really want to hear any counter arguments. They are not open to new ideas. This sort of repels people who approach with an open and logical mind."	"I do not feel any discontent with my agnosticism. I am open-minded and am always up for a learning experience, but I do not feel as though I am missing anything in my life."	"I believe in a higher power, but I'm not really sure if that is God, or time or universe. It does kinda suck being this confused, but I suppose it doesn't bother me."	"I have questions about the numerous religions and which one is closest to actuality, have a hard time believing anyone has it exactly right."	"To me, religion is a man-made construct to control the populous. Unfortunately, it uses faith and spirituality of people to manipulate them for monetary, land, and power advancements. Faith is something you believe in, not something you are told to believe in."	"I do believe there is a God I believe I was created by God and can communicate with Him through prayer and listen to His words. At times, I feel that I am disappointed with myself when I failed to reach the target."	"My spiritual goal in life is to follow the path of Jesus, trying to live with the beliefs of what's good and moral and trying to help those who are still looking for something or someone to believe in."

Figure 2. Infographic of Seven Personas. Brooke Wright et al. *Understanding Faith and Purpose in the City*. Atlanta: Cyrano Marketing Collective, 2016. Copyright Cru, 2018. Reprinted with permission.[22]

These personas revealed a continuum of belief consistent with the Scripture. On the left, Jen, an *antidogmatic*, contends that religious people, held captive by their own beliefs, lack the ability to engage in robust discussion. Next to Jen is Alan, who is *unaware* and *content* and basically sees no need for religion. Danielle, the *anxious* yet *curious* persona, believes in the possibility of a higher power, but is bewildered. She wonders how to determine who or what that higher power is. Aarón, the *explorer*, is aware of various religious options, but questions which one is right. Crystal describes herself as *disillusioned*. In her view, religion is simply a man-made theory used to control people and obtain wealth. Wes is *inquisitive,* and as a *progressive,* he believes in God who has created him for a purpose. On the far right of the scale is Shawn who is *faithful*; he actively follows Jesus and helps others follow him too

---

[22]   Wright et al.

We also discovered a simple Scale of Belief (see figure 3).[23] From left to right: the *unaware*—those who are unconcerned about religion, spirituality, or God; the *curious*—those who are willing and open to conversation; the *content*—those who find life satisfying, willingly give of themselves, but feel no need for God. On the right hand of the scale, we find those who identify as *followers, activators,* or *guides* and actively follow God and involve others.

The Scale of Belief

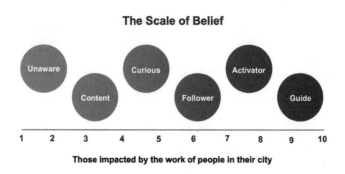

Those impacted by the work of people in their city

Figure 3. Infographic of the Scale of Belief. Brooke Wright et al. *Understanding Faith and Purpose in the City*. Atlanta: Cyrano Marketing Collective, 2016. Copyright Cru, 2018. Reprinted with permission.

Importantly, the Scale of Belief that emerged is consistent with Scripture and evidenced in the many interactions Jesus had with all kinds of people during his earthly ministry. In chapter 4 we return to some of these very encouraging discoveries, but until then, we move to vantage point 3.

---

[23] Wright et al.

Missiological Vantage Point 3:
Demographic Changes and a Diversity Explosion

America's changing demographics provide another important reason for reimagining gospel conversations.[24] Demographer William Frey considers this "sweep of diversity" an important landmark. Frey compares the white baby-boom culture of the late twentieth century to today's increasingly globalized and multiracial population. He states, "I am convinced that the United States is in the midst of a pivotal period ushering in extraordinary shifts in the nation's racial demographic makeup," and contends that immigration plays a significant role in this diversity explosion.[25]

Abby Budiman of the Pew Research Center underscores this point. She reports that an astonishing 1 million immigrants arrive in the United States each year, more than in any other country in the world, and estimates that 40 million people living in the United States were born in another country.[26] She notes, "Since 1965, when U.S. immigration laws replaced a national quota system, the number of immigrants living in the U.S. has more than quadrupled. Immigrants today account for 13.7% of the U.S. population, nearly triple the share in (4.8%) in 1970."[27] Budiman's research suggests that by 2055, the number of Asian immigrants will surpass the number of Hispanic immigrants.[28] Importantly, this diversity explosion creates complexity and introduces new and different attitudes and

---

[24] William H. Frey, *Diversity Explosion: How New Racial Demographics are Remaking America* (Washington, DC: Brookings Institution Press, 2015), 5.

[25] Frey, *Diversity Explosion*, 3.

[26] Abby Budiman, "Key Findings About U.S. Immigrants," Pew Research Center, August 20, 2020, https://www.pewresearch.org/short-reads/2020/08/20/key-findings-about-u-s-immigrants/.

[27] Budiman.

[28] Budiman.

worldviews that affect many aspects of life, including institutional and political practices in the US.

This sweep of diversity in America's population naturally includes various worldviews related to sociology and religion. Linda Bergquist and Michael Crane assert, "We are living in a time between the times when worldviews are in transition. Many of the tensions and disagreements in the world today can be at least partially attributed to this worldview transition . . . a shift from modern to emerging worldview values."[29] They point out, "Respect for and protection of diversity is one of the most significant worldviews emerging at this time. The idea of diversity resonates with pluralism and the realization that the planet is amazingly interconnected."[30]

They also posit that while most American Christians have received some training in evangelism, most are woefully unprepared to engage in a gospel conversation with hyper-spiritual Hindus, Buddhists, Sikhs, or Muslims. This sweep of diversity provides the church with new opportunities to train and equip Christians to engage in meaningful gospel conversations with family, friends, coworkers, and neighbors who hold entirely different points of view.

Missiological Vantage Point 4: Gen Z, the Next Generation

This vantage point focuses on Gen Z—the post-Millennial generation—which includes those born between 1999 and 2015.[31] Barna Group, in 2018, set out to discover the ethos, viewpoints, and

---

[29] Linda Bergquist and Michael D. Crane, *City Shaped Churches: Planting Churches in the Global Era* (Skyforest, CA: Urban Loft, 2018), 103.

[30] Bergquist and Crane, 206.

[31] Barna Group, *Gen Z: The Culture, Beliefs and Motivations Shaping the Next Generation* (Ventura, CA: Barna Group, 2018), 10.

motivations shared by Gen Z, by surveying teenagers, Christian parents, youth workers, and pastors.[32] The report provides a summary of Gen Z's worldview and, by doing so, helps to highlight the differences between Bill Bright's context and ours today.

On the one hand, these findings serve us missiologically by uncovering aspects of Gen Z's worldview, the roots of their identity, their experience with diversity, and their beliefs about truth and morality. On the other hand, this section underscores the significance of contextualization. For instance, the fact that no one worldview describes Gen Z requires us to consider gospel witness today from a very different vantage point. The prevailing question in 1951, "Is it true?" is being replaced by the question, "Why does Jesus matter?" Barna Group's qualitative analysis included two focus groups with U.S. teenagers between the ages of 14 and 17. The first included teenagers whose parents considered their child a Christian ("Christian Group"), and the second consisted entirely of teenagers who parents do not consider their child a Christian ("Non-Christian" group)".

Gen Z's Worldview
Important for our discussion, Barna Group's research illustrates the effects of an increasingly secularized context. "Out of 69 million children and teens in Gen Z, just four percent have a biblical worldview."[33] In addition, and somewhat surprisingly, of those who do identify as Christian, only one in eleven claims to follow Jesus as a

---

[32]   Barna Group, 111. Barna's qualitative analysis included two focus groups with U.S. teenagers between the ages of 14 and 17. The first included teenagers whose parents considered their child a Christian ("Christian Group"), and the second consisted entirely of teenagers who parents do not consider their child a Christian ("Non-Christian" group)".
[33]   Barna Group, 13.

way of life. While many adhere to atheism, still more are captivated by some kind of spirituality.

Barna Group's hopeful claim that Gen Z is a "spiritual blank slate,"[34] however, is misleading and contradicts their research. For example, they assert that "social media is completely reinventing what it means to come of age as a teenager,"[35] and highlight the powerful influence of the internet on various facets of life, including worldview and mental health. In his book *Meet Generation Z*, James Emery White quotes author, researcher, and missiologist Ed Stetzer on the changing context of our current culture: "As the cultural cost of being a Christian increases, people who were once Christian in name only likely have started to identify as nones, disintegrating the 'ideological bridge' between unbelievers and believers."[36] We must not underestimate the formative power of social media on Gen Z's view of the world—and our own.

GEN Z: IDENTITY AND DIVERSITY

Barna Group's findings suggest that Gen Z's identity and world-view is shaped by their commitment to inclusion and individualism. "Their collective aversion to causing offense is the natural product of a pluralistic, inclusive culture that frowns on passing judgment that might provoke negative feelings in the judged."[37] Their commit-ment to accept and affirm all people is illustrated, for example, by their fluid viewpoints on gender and sexuality. However, Tim Elmore points out that the complexity of sexual and gender identity can lead

---

[34] Barna Group, 10.

[35] Barna Group, 5.

[36] James Emery White, *Meet Generation Z: Understanding and Reaching the New Post-Christian World* (Grand Rapids: Baker, 2017), 32.

[37] Barna Group, *Gen Z*, 27.

to heightened anxiety and other serious mental health issues. "This generation of children and teens suffer more from mental health problems than any other generation of kids in American history."[38] Elmore, attentive to the significance of mental health today, suggests that Gen Z needs positive reinforcement and opportunities to escape negative interaction.

Barna Group reports that diversity adds another facet to Gen Z's worldview. The fact that 50 percent of the respondents are not white means that this generation constitutes "the most racially, religiously and sexually diverse generation in American history."[39] Gen Z, having grown up in multiracial and diverse families and structures, naturally values diversity. Furthermore, "For them diversity is not just about race; it's a complex intersection of values, language, culture, family structures, interpersonal dynamics, customs, finances and education."[40] These findings add texture to the demographic changes in America mentioned earlier.

Gen Z: Morality, Values, and Truth
Gen Z's view of morality reflects moral relativism—the belief that morality is dynamic and always changing. Said one teen in a Barna focus group, "Society changes and what's good or bad changes as well. It is all relative to what's happening in the world."[41] Consequently, this generation holds progressive or liberal views on subjects like gender, sexuality, and abortion. This relative view of

---

[38] Tim Elmore and Andrew McPeak, *Generation Z: Unfiltered* (Atlanta: Poet Gardner, 2019), loc. 575 of 5705, Kindle.

[39] Barna Group, *Gen Z*, 12.

[40] Barna Group, 31.

[41] Barna Group, 56.

morality, developed in a secularized context without any reference to God, is crucial for us to understand.

Gen Z values are reflected in their desire to make a difference in the world. On the one hand, they actively care about local and global issues like gun control and climate change.[42] On the other hand, they view the church and religion as irrelevant, and faith in God as nonsensical. For most, truth, like morality, "seems relative at best and, at worst, altogether unknowable."[43] To make matters worse, unsatisfactory answers to their questions about the existence of God and evil further substantiate the irrelevance of religion.[44] Not surprisingly, the research also shows that while 58 percent believe in some kind of afterlife, most reject the idea of one true religion.

Reflection

I began this chapter with a provocative question: "If it was so easy to believe in God in 1951, why is it so hard today?" and introduced four missiological vantage points to lend insight into the contrast between Bright's context and ours today. Secularization, Cru's research, demographics and diversity, and Gen Z provide windows into our twenty-first-century context and underscore the need to

---

[42] Elmore and McPeak (*Generation Z*, loc. 822 of 5705, Kindle) note that on March 24, 2018, 400,000 teenagers took part in March for Our Lives, a protest against gun violence in response to a school shooting at Marjory Stoneman Douglas High School in Parkland, Florida, where seventeen students were killed on February 14, 2018.

Greta Thunberg, a Swedish-born environmental activist, at the age of fifteen, addressed the United Nations in August 2018 and consequently influenced student strikes around the world.

[43] Barna Group, *Gen Z*, 64.

[44] Barna Group, 64.

better understand our culture so that we can reimagine meaningful gospel conversations.

I had the opportunity, just a year after I graduated with my PhD, to speak at a chapel gathering at a well-known Christian university. After I finished my presentation, I engaged with students around their observations and questions. I also spent quite a while with two students who took issue with my description of Gen Z, their generation.

These two students, one who was African American, and one who identified as queer, questioned my approach from their respective points of view. They understood me to say that America's changing demographics in today's context are *bad* and that we should return to the predominantly white population of the 1950s. They described my portrayal of their generation as off-putting and reminded me that they are not just measured and researched statistics but are people whose voices matter in these conversations.

I left that auditorium sobered by their misunderstandings and grateful for their initiative and input. On the one hand, I realized that I need to explain myself with greater care and attention to my audience, and on the other hand, I need to consider the assumptions and potential misperceptions people might have related to my ethnicity, gender, and age. Significantly, I realized in a new way the importance of being a learner and continue to engage in conversations with people who represent different generations, including Gen Z. I'll cover more about being a learner in a later chapter.

In chapter 3, I introduce the True Story of the Whole World (True Story) and describe how my research into the metanarrative of Scripture helped me to find my balance amid the shifts I have been describing. I discovered that God's gospel is strong and resilient.

Finding Our Bearings in the True Story of the Whole World

A s my disorientation continued in the early 2000s, I was tempted to give up sharing my faith altogether, but God persistently exposed me to people from a host of different backgrounds and beliefs who actively engaged with me in meaningful and often deep spiritual conversations. These encounters happened so frequently that I could not help but pay attention. I started to listen more closely and to initiate a conversation rather than feel the pressure to make a presentation. I learned (and am still learning) to value each person and their story.

One memorable conversation took place on a flight from Raleigh, North Carolina, to Orlando, Florida, when Isa, a high school graduate from the United Kingdom, happened to sit next to me. She freely described her summer vacation and looked forward to a few days at Disney World before heading back home to start college. She planned to study microbiology. She then wondered the reason for my trip to Orlando, so I explained that I was headed to Orlando for work. She inquired further. I told her that I work for Cru, a faith-based organization headquartered there. Her friendly, inquisitive posture changed dramatically at the mention of "faith based." I hesitated to say more. But deep down I wondered—what prompted her strong reaction? So, I gently asked what caused her negative reaction and posed a question, "Would you be willing to tell me more?" For the next hour, she shared her journey of faith.

Isa explained that her favorite aunt had recently passed away due to cancer. Tears welled in her eyes as she explained that she begged God to let her aunt live. And, as her aunt's condition worsened, she pleaded with God to take her life instead of her aunt's. Sadly, her aunt passed away.

As she shared her story, memories of my mom's untimely death flooded my mind. I related to Isa how I lost my mom due to brain cancer when I was in my late twenties. I could relate to the depth of her pain and loss because, like Isa's aunt, my mom lived only a few short months after her diagnosis. I identified with her longing to take her aunt's place in death. I knew the ache of watching a loved one suffer in agony and then die. I shared how much my mom depended on God's love for her, for me, and for our family during that time, and how much God helped our family during those dark days. I could not help but share the parallel between God's love for us and her love for her aunt. God knows the pain of sending his only Son to die in our place.

As our flight descended into Orlando, I shared a few verses with her from Scripture and wrote them down on my business card. As quickly as the conversation started, it shifted, and we parted ways. As I rolled my bag off the plane, I waved goodbye to Isa with an overwhelming sense of God's love for her and for me. Jesus says, "No one can come to me unless the Father who sent me draws him" (John 6:44), and I am convinced he is drawing Isa to himself. It was clear from our conversation that there are several Jesus followers in her life. Significantly, God often reminds me to pray for her and to pray for the believers whose paths will cross hers—encounters orchestrated by God.

As conversations like the one I had with Isa continued to happen, I listened and watched more for the Spirit's leading and paid closer attention to each person I encountered. Around the same time, as my approach to engaging in meaningful gospel conversations became increasingly discombobulated, I explored the possibility of attending seminary. Little did I know that the decade between my fiftieth and sixtieth birthdays would be marked by master's and doctoral research that sifted and sorted my ordered view of God and the gospel, and would also reshape my approach to meaningful gospel conversations in profound ways.

The purpose of this chapter is twofold. First, I introduce a simple framework for understanding the Bible as the True Story of the Whole World (True Story) and a brief description of the four key themes found in the True Story. Second, I provide a missional theology that centers on God—the creator of the universe, and on the mission of God—the *missio Dei*. I wrap up this chapter by providing two cultural fables or counternarratives at play all around us to illustrate the significance of the True Story in a pervasively secularized context.

The True Story of the Whole World: The Metanarrative of Scripture

My first semester in seminary included four classes, two of which transformed my understanding of the Bible: Old Testament (OT) Survey and Hermeneutics. The required reading for the OT class included the first thirty-nine books of the Bible and for the

Hermeneutics class, *The True Story of the Whole World: Finding Your Place in the Biblical Drama.*[1]

Until seminary, quite honestly, I had read the Bible from beginning to end only a few times. I had been taught to "master the Bible a book at a time." For years I had studied and taught specific books in the OT and New Testament (NT), and by the time I entered seminary, I had even written numerous Bible studies on various NT epistles. But it was the combination of those two classes that helped me to identify the metanarrative of Scripture and enriched my understanding of God, the Scriptures, and the gospel. I discovered that the sixty-six books of the Bible combine to tell the true story of the whole world and clarify the mission of God, the *missio Dei*, along familiar themes like Creation, Rebellion, Redemption, and New Creation.[2]

For example, I found inklings of the gospel in God's grace and provision for Abraham and Sarah and discovered echoes of God's deliverance in the nation of Israel. The Song of Moses put music to faint echoes of God's Son crucified and crowned. I began to hear the steady note of God's love and redemption reverberating across the story and into the lives of Hagar, Rahab, and Ruth. God's inexplicable mercy comes to life through a little slave girl who speaks up on behalf of a leper. His grace and mercy spill out from Israel's borders, reaching pagans like Nebuchadnezzar and saving pagan

---

[1]   Craig G. Bartholomew and Michael W. Goheen, *The True Story of the Whole World: Finding Your Place in the Biblical Drama* (Grand Rapids: Faith Alive, 2004).

[2]   Christopher J. H. Wright, *The Great Story and the Great Commission: Participating in the Biblical Drama of Mission* (Grand Rapids: Baker Academic, 2023), 33. I follow Wright's lead and describe the fourth key theme of Scripture as the "New Creation" rather than "Restoration" or "Re-creation." Wright describes the New Creation as "the glory of ultimate redemption and restoration.… the great biblical *hope*—using that word in its full biblical sense. That is, this is not merely something we would like to think *might* happen. This is what we confidently expect *will* happen, because of the certainty of the promises of God and the guarantee of Christ's resurrection" (p. 33).

nations. The deep timbre of forgiveness transforms the lives of people like David and Bathsheba in the OT and Mary Magdalene and Paul in the NT.

I noticed hints of the Suffering Servant in Isaiah's songs, and as I made my way to the NT, the incarnation leapt off the pages! God the Son, through the incarnation, took on human flesh and lived and died in our place. Foundationally, the Bible reminds us, God will make his name known. "For the earth will be filled with the knowledge of the LORD's glory, as the water covers the sea" (Hab 2:14), and "For God who said, 'Let light shine out of darkness,' has shone in our hearts to give the light of the knowledge of God's glory in the face of Jesus Christ" (2 Cor 4:6).

God began showing me through the whole story of Scripture that God's mission is comprehensive. Everywhere we go, everything we are part of, every conversation is orchestrated by God. God's Spirit puts us in touch with baristas and barbers, lawyers and engineers, professors and Uber drivers, and calls us to be his witnesses. I began to realize that our evangelistic encounters must be framed by our telling of the Bible's overarching story, its grand narrative.

The True Story: The Drama of Scripture

Around this same time, I received as a gift Sally Lloyd-Jones's *The Jesus Storybook Bible: Every Story Whispers His Name*.[3] The beautifully illustrated pages drew me into the story as God's Spirit reminded me that God never stops and never gives up. His always and forever love resounds from creation to the new creation.

I also began to look at the four prominent themes found in the Bible—Creation, Rebellion, Redemption, and New Creation—which

---

[3] Sally Lloyd-Jones, *The Jesus Storybook Bible: Every Story Whispers His Name* (Grand Rapids: Zondervan, 2007).

provide for us simple summaries of a rather lengthy and complex story. *The True Story of the Whole World* introduced the True Story with six acts. These include Act 1: God Establishes the Kingdom (Creation); Act 2: Rebellion in the Kingdom (the Fall); Act 3: The King Chooses Israel (Redemption Initiated); Act 4: The Coming of the King (Redemption Accomplished); Act 5: Spreading the News of the King; and Act 6: Return of the King.[4]

The four key themes and six acts illustrate an overarching unity of purpose and help us to better understand God, the nation of Israel, and the relationship between the OT and the NT. In other words, the Bible contains sixty-six books that include a variety of genres written by many different authors over the course of thousands of years. At the heart of this story is Jesus, in whom God reveals his fullest purpose and meaning for human history . . . and consequently provides the meaning of your life and mine.

The following section provides a summary of the four key themes that run through the True Story from the beginning of the Bible to the end: Creation, Rebellion, Redemption, and New Creation. I provide key passages for easy reference.

Creation

Genesis, the first book of Scripture, begins with the creation story. We learn in the first few verses that the triune God spoke the heavens and the earth into existence out of nothing. God called the light into

---

[4] Bartholomew and Goheen, *The True Story of the Whole World*, Table of Contents. N. T. Wright's *Scripture and the Authority of God: How to Read the Bible Today* (New York: HarperOne, 2013) tells the story in five acts: Act 1: Creation; Act 2: Fall; Act 3: Israel; Act 4: Jesus; and Act 5 posits that the story continues to be told through the church until the New Creation. Christopher Wright, *The Great Story,* suggests that seven key themes resound across Scripture: Creation, Rebellion, Promise, Christ, Mission, Judgment, and New Creation, 33.

existence and separates light from dark. He gathered the waters into one place and created the dry land from which sprouted seeds and plants, trees and fruit. He created swarms of living creatures, including birds to fly above the earth and beasts and livestock to live on the earth (Gen 1:25). Then, God planted a garden: "The LORD God planted a garden in Eden, in the east, and there he placed the man he had formed. The LORD God caused to grow out of the ground every tree pleasing in appearance and good for food (Gen 2:8–9a).

The pinnacle of God's creation is man and woman created in God's image or likeness for relationship with God, self, others, and the created world. Humankind, sent by God and set apart to function as God "imagers," tend the garden.[5] "Then God said, 'Let us make man in our image, according to our likeness. They will rule the fish of the sea, the birds of the sky, the livestock, the whole earth, and the creatures that crawl on the earth.'… God blessed them, and God said to them, 'Be fruitful, multiply, fill the earth, and subdue it'" (Gen 1:26, 28a; see also Gen 1:26–31; 2:21–24; and Psalm 8).

We further recognize the functional and relational aspect of *imago Dei* demonstrated through people like Abram, who is blessed by God and through whom God will bless the families of the earth (Gen 12:1–3); Moses, whom God raises up as a deliverer to lead Israel out of Egyptian bondage (Exod 3:7–12); David, who reigns as king over the nation of Israel, through whom God will establish his

---

[5]   Bruce Riley Ashford and Heath A. Thomas, *The Gospel of Our King: Bible, Worldview, and the Mission of Every Christian* (Grand Rapids: Baker Academic, 2019), 19–25. The meaning of *imago Dei* is mysterious and contested. Ashford and Thomas's analysis is instructive and provides a well-researched overview of different arguments related to *imago Dei*, beginning with the church fathers followed by Martin Luther, John Calvin, Karl Barth, up to the present day. Ashford and Thomas's treatment of the topic is well worth the read.

kingdom (2 Sam 7:5–17); and Ruth, who shows compassion for her mother-in-law (Ruth 1:6–18).

Bruce Ashford and Heath Thomas state, "The image of God is not a property of humanity, as if one could take it off like a coat. Instead, it is a given."[6] *Imago Dei* is integral to our makeup and constitution and represents the handiwork of God at the very core of our being. The psalmist thus worships the Creator's fearful and wonderful works:

> For you formed my inward parts;
> you knitted me together in my mother's womb.
> I praise you, for I am fearfully and wonderfully made.
> Wonderful are your works;
> my soul knows it very well.
> My frame was not hidden from you,
> when I was being made in secret,
> intricately woven in the depths of the earth.
> Your eyes saw my unformed substance;
> in your book were written, every one of them,
> the days that were formed for me,
> when as yet there was none of them. (Ps 139:13–16 ESV)

Likewise, Paul reminds us that "we are his workmanship, created in Christ Jesus for good works, which God prepared ahead of time for us to do" (Eph 2:10).

The creation story, sometimes in veiled ways, introduces us to the triune God (the Father, Son, and Spirit), the King, who reigns in sovereignty over the cosmos. God, who acts in creation from Genesis to Revelation, is worthy of our worship. The whole earth, right

---

[6] Ashford and Thomas, *Gospel of Our King,* 22.

now and continuously, worships and adores God the Creator for his ongoing love and care for the kingdom that he created. The Bible reminds us that God's glory is declared from the highest heavens to the ends of the earth. The deserts and mountains shout for joy and the morning stars sing. All of God's creation agonizes for and eagerly anticipates the revelation of the sons of God. Throughout Scripture, God's imagers honor and worship and praise God's name, for even in the face of great suffering, God is our helper who can always be found in times of trouble. He listens to our cries, he is our protector and provider, his faithful love never comes to an end (Job 38–42; Psalms 45; 77; 86; 92; 96; 103; Isa 49:13; Rom 8:18–21).

We tend to refer to God the Creator in the past tense: "*In the beginning*—a very long time ago—God created the world." However, we must remember that God rules and reigns in the universe right now (Job 38–42; Pss 89:1–10; 95:1–7). Yes, God spoke the creation into existence at a specific point in time, but we must not overlook God's comprehensive participation in, and his authority over, creation still today. Jesus demonstrates his power over creation throughout his ministry. He turns water to wine, walks on water, feeds 5,000, calms the winds and the seas, gives sight to the blind, heals all sorts of diseases, and raises the dead (John 2:1–12; 4:46–54; 5:1–17; 6:1–21; 9:1–12; 11:17–44). On the one hand, the heavens declare the glory of God and the earth is full of God's creatures who worship him and depend on him for food, and on the other hand, the whole creation groans as it waits to be set free from its bondage to corruption and to obtain the freedom of the glory of the children of God (Ps 47:5–7; 33:6–9; 89:1–11; 104; Rom 8:18–25).

Rebellion

Within a short period of time, the idyllic creation story was disrupted. Adam and Eve dare to rebel against God, their Creator,

49

setting into motion a devastating sequence of events. God provided clear instruction from the very beginning—work and maintain the garden, be fruitful and multiply, and do not eat from the tree of knowledge—God's only prohibition. "But you must not eat from the tree of the knowledge of good and evil, for on the day you eat from it, you will certainly die" (Gen 2:17). Adam and Eve, tempted by the serpent, doubted God's love, questioned God's goodness, and ultimately disobeyed God's authority. This one choice shattered their relationship with God and wreaked havoc in their marriage and on their family. God created Adam and Eve for meaning and purpose, but rebellion plummeted them into conflict (Gen 3:22–4:16).[7]

The storyline of Scripture reverberates with the comprehensive effects of sin. Within a very short time, it becomes apparent that the effects of sin penetrate every individual, every family, and even earthly systems, evidenced at the Tower of Babel (Gen 11:1–8). The psalmist laments, "The Lord looks down from heaven on the human race to see if there is one who is wise, one who seeks God. All have turned away; all alike have become corrupt. There is no one who does good, not even one" (Ps 14:2–3; see also Ps 53:1–3), and verifies that "no one alive is righteous" (Ps 143:2). The prophet Isaiah confirms that evil and injustice prevail because of sin (Isa 59:7–9, 12). Jeremiah declares, "The heart is more deceitful than anything else, and incurable" (Jer 17:9). Eventually, the apostle Paul agrees, "For all have sinned and fall short of the glory of God" (Rom 3:23). The effect of Adam's sin is cosmic. God's creation is subject to futility and bound by decay (Rom 8:20–21).

Affirming the cosmic effects of sin, bleak as that seems, unlocks the deeper meaning of the True Story. The Scriptures make it clear that sin—all wickedness and perversion across all time—is

---

[7]   Notably, this rebellion against God began with Lucifer the archangel and the heavenly host who joined him (Gen 3:1–13; Isaiah 14).

ultimately the result of humankind's refusal to live under the Creator's rule, evidenced still today in our secularized and humanist culture (Gen 2:17; Pss 14:2–3; 53:1–3; 143:2; Isa 59:7–9, 12; Romans 1–3; Eph 2:1–10; Gal 1:1–5; Col 2:8–15).

Redemption

The good news is that God's love remains true even in spite of Adam and Eve's rebellion. Though God expels them from the garden, He does not abandon them. In fact, Genesis 3:15, sometimes referred to as the first gospel, provides a hint of God's redemption. Here, God promises that through the offspring of the woman, Satan will be dealt a fatal blow.

As the story unfolds, it becomes clear that all of humanity, both objects and agents of God's mission, will also become participants in the *missio Dei*. Early in Genesis, God actively uses all kinds of people to restore the broken world and to accomplish his redemptive purposes. For example, Noah, called by God, obeys, and builds an ark (Gen 6:1–8:19). His obedience preserves his family, "his sons, his wife, and his son's wives," and "all the animals, all the creatures that crawl, and all the flying creatures—everything that moves on the earth" from the cataclysmic flood (Gen 8:18–19). Then, after the waters subside, God promises, "I will never again curse the ground because of human beings" (Gen 8:21). God enters into a covenant with Noah and commissions him to "be fruitful and multiply and fill the earth" (Gen 9:1).

Next, God calls Abraham away from his home and makes a promise: "I will make you into a great nation, I will bless you, I will make your name great, and you will be a blessing" (Gen 12:2). Some twenty-five years later, Abraham and Sarah, now "as good as dead" (Rom 4:19 NIV), finally embrace the fulfillment of God's promise in their son Isaac (Gen 21:1–3). Then, in a dark plot twist,

God asks Abraham to sacrifice his son, and Abraham responds in obedience and by faith binds Isaac for sacrifice. But God provides a substitute and redeems Isaac, and Abraham is justified by faith, foreshadowing justification by faith in Jesus Christ (Gen 22:1–19; Rom 4:1–4; Gal 3:6–9).

Likewise, God delivers Moses and the nation of Israel out of Egyptian bondage. Then, at Mount Sinai, God commissions them to be a kingdom of priests and a light to the nations (Exod 19:1–6; Isa 42:6; 49:6; 51:4). God's covenant with Moses foreshadows God's provision of a prophet from among their brothers (Deut 18:15–18). God also initiates the Law and establishes the Levitical priesthood to carry out the administration of atoning sacrifices (Exodus 20–39). Later in the story, God will send Jesus Christ as the final and ulti-mate sacrifice once and for all time. Jesus Christ is the last prophet, the perfect High Priest, the better gift and sacrifice, and the victori-ous King (Heb 4:14–16; 9–11; in particular, Heb 9:11–15).

In time, Israel demands an earthly king, and God concedes to Israel's appeal and appoints Saul as ruler over Israel. Saul is even-tually rejected by God because of his rebellion. God then anoints David in his place and establishes a covenant therein promising to establish his throne forever (1 Sam 8:5; 10:1; 16:12–13; 2 Sam 7:4–17). David's earthly reign foreshadows the ultimate reign of Jesus Christ.

Later in Israel's history, before the Babylonian captivity, the prophet Isaiah describes a Suffering Servant, who will be clothed with the garments of salvation and robes of righteousness, will bring redemption, judge in righteousness, and vanquish sin and death (Isa 42:1–9; 49; 50; 52:13–53:12; 54:8–9; 61).

The New Testament opens with an astonishing event—the incarnation. God the Son, clothed in human flesh, accomplishes redemption (Luke 1:26–55). Jesus, the Son of Man, heralds the good news—the inbreaking of God's kingdom. He assures the crowds, "The Son of Man did not come to be served, but to serve, and to give his life as a ransom for many" (Matt 20:28). He purposes to restore everything lost in the fall, including humankind's relationship with God. Jesus Christ, the Suffering Servant, atoned for sin through his precious blood on the cross and defeated sin and death through the resurrection (John 10:7–18; 12:23–24, 31–33; Rom 1:18–3:20; Hebrews 9–10; 1 Pet 1:17–20). Jesus Christ is the image of the invisible God, the firstborn of all creation and the firstborn from the dead, who redeems and reconciles all things to God (Romans 4–8; Col 1:15–23; 1 Pet 1:13–21).

In the hours before the cross, Jesus gathered the disciples for the Passover meal and to prepare them for his imminent death and departure. He is returning to his Father's house to prepare a place for them (John 13:1; 14:1–3) and reassures them that the Father is sending another Counselor, the Spirit of truth, who will remain with them forever (John 14:15–31; 20:22; Acts 1:7–8).

Jesus promises his disciples that God's Spirit provides power for a flourishing life, an otherworldly peace and hope, freedom from anxiety and fear, and the courage to be his witnesses in the face of hatred and opposition (John 10:10; John 14:25–31; 15:18–25; 16:5–11, 33; Acts 1:8; Rom 8:1–11; Eph 3:14–21). God's original design in Genesis will come to fruition in the new creation (Revelation 20–21). In the meantime, Jesus reminds them that through the Spirit's divine power they have everything they need for life and godliness (Eph 1:11–14; 2 Pet 1:3–4)

God also sends the Spirit to empower and invigorate the church in the *missio Dei*. The church, in turn, bears witness to the good news and carries it to the nations. This community, filled with individuals who are chosen by God to be part of his family, flourishes and finds meaning as it participates in God's mission. This whole new way of life was evidenced in the early church as believers sold their belongings and shared their possessions to help those in need (Acts 2:42–46). They established leadership to guide and instruct the church (Acts 15; 18–20; 1 Thess 1:1–2; 1 Tim 3; 5:17–25) and learned to prioritize the care of widows and orphans (1 Tim 5:1–16; Jas 1:27).

The magnificence of redemption, through the resurrection of Jesus Christ, brings radical, transformational change now and looks ahead with hope to the new heavens and new earth as God's dwelling with humanity (Rom 8:18–25; Ephesians 1–3; Col 1:15–20; 1 Peter 1–2; Rev 21:1–4).

New Creation

The true story of the whole world begins in Genesis with God's creation of the heavens and the earth and climaxes in Revelation with the new creation (Revelation 20–21). The good news reaches back to Genesis and promises redemption and hope for humankind and all of God's creation. The Bible reiterates and even brings to life God's promise to make all things new now and at the end of the age (Isa 65:17–25; Ezek 36:26; Heb 10:19–22; 12:26–27; 2 Pet 3:4–13; Revelation 21–22). Furthermore, the fruit of this new creation, triumphantly declared in Christ, is comprehensive in scope and anticipates God's promised healing and redemption, fullness and flourishing.

Jesus Christ, the plumb line of God's story, embodies the new creation in triumph through his resurrection. "He is the image of the invisible God, the firstborn over all creation . . . . He is the beginning, the firstborn from the dead, so that he might come to have first place in everything" (Col 1:15, 18; see also Rom 5:12–20; 1 Cor 15:3–5, 12–23). Jesus Christ, through his death, burial, and resurrection, establishes a new covenant and a new commandment and thereby makes all things new, including us (Luke 22:20; John 13:34; Rom 6:1–4; 8:9–11; 1 Cor 15:42–49; 2 Cor 5:16–17; 6:16–18; Gal 6:15; Eph 2:4–10; Col 3:9–10; 1 Pet 1:1–5; 1 John 1:7–9).

As God's children, we are free to forgive sacrificially, to love selflessly, to practice radical generosity in the face of injustice and opposition. The church, until Christ returns, is God's visible manifestation of the transformation from death to life, old to new, creation to new creation (Matt 5:1–12; Luke 6:17–26; Acts 4:32–37; 2 Cor 8:9; Eph 4:17–32; Phil 2:1–12; Colossians 3–4; Heb 6:12–20; 1 Pet 2:9–24; 3:8–15; 4:1–5:11).

These four key themes provide for us a theological framework of the True Story and enable us to recognize the mission of God all the way through Scripture. The comprehensive nature of the True Story helped me find my balance and gave me confidence to actively research and interact with the cultural shifts and disruptions I was experiencing. In the next section, I provide two examples of cultural fables that shed light on our changing culture: "God Is a Woman," and "The Universe Has Your Back." I demonstrate how to analyze these examples in light of the True Story and how to engage in meaningful ways.

Cultural Fables and Counternarratives

Engaging in meaningful gospel conversations with our friends and neighbors, if we are paying attention, can increase our awareness of the prevalence of secularization. These conversations can also lend insight into the significance of the True Story. Remember, Taylor's secularization considers belief in God not only implausible but unimaginable and is based entirely on what can be explained or experienced without any reference to God. Importantly, this secularization is rife with belief and treats Christianity as one option among an explosion of others.

Today's secularization challenges traditional assumptions and conditions of belief regarding not only faith and God, but also history, morality, rationality, identity, and society. We see evidence of this today, for example, in society's preoccupation with deconstruction, cancel culture, and the rise of the *nones*.[8] Compare this twenty-first-century secularization with Bill Bright's mid-twentieth-century context introduced in chapter 1.

So, I have purposefully chosen to use the phrase True Story of the Whole World, in today's context, to reinforce the fact that the metanarrative of Scripture is not just one among the many religious stories out there; it is neither a myth nor a preferred story that competes with other religious stories. The key themes of Creation, Rebellion, Redemption, and New Creation serve to tell a story that is universally true, is historically embedded (it really happened), and provides a framework of meaning for your life and mine. This bold claim stands out in a secularized culture where truth is relativized. It gives us confidence as we interact with people in our families, neighborhoods, workplaces, and cities.

I emphasize this because there are other narratives at work out there in our culture and society that might look and feel true, but instead, they challenge the veracity of the True Story. Sometimes these false claims are immediately obvious, brazen, and offensive. Other times, they are subtle and alluring forgeries tempting us to believe a divergent narrative. I am convinced that we must heighten our awareness of the True Story to better recognize the counterfeit

---

[8] "'Nones' on the Rise," The Pew Research Center, October 9, 2012, https://www.pewresearch.org/religion/2012/10/09/nones-on-the-rise/. The Pew Research Center describes "nones" as those who identify as religiously unaffiliated.

claims, the cultural fables that compete for our collective attention and devotion.

"God Is a Woman"

Ulta Beauty is an American chain store that carries perfumes, cosmetics, and personal care products all under one roof. I shop at Ulta once every few months for my beauty necessities and receive their monthly ad magazine that often includes three or four fragrance samples. Recently, a little perfume square floated from the magazine down to my counter promoting a new fragrance developed by pop artist Ariana Grande called "God is a Woman." I was not familiar with Grande's music or artistry, but "God is a Woman" caught my eye, so I decided to do a little research.

First, I learned that the bold assertion, "God is a woman," is borrowed from Grande's 2018 hit single with the same title. While the music video and lyrics are way too steamy for me, I was interested to learn that the music video for this song, in which she appears as various deities, pays tribute to Greek mythology, the female body, and Romulus and Remus from Roman mythology. Added to the cacophony is Michelangelo's fresco, *The Creation of Adam*. Included in her depiction of "god," she references the Day of the Lord and features a Madonna voice-over loosely quoting a passage from Ezekiel. These spiritual overtones and gross misunderstandings of the Day of the Lord represent Taylor's galloping pluralism. Grande, aware that the assertion "God is a woman" might stir some controversy, insists that her music is a work of art whether people understand or agree with what she creates or not.

My intention here is not to lambaste Grande for her assumptions, but instead to highlight a pop-culture counternarrative and to consider the opportunity it presents. What does her choice of words and imagery teach us about the cultural narratives of our secular age, and how does this story line up with the True Story? How does this fable shed light on our need to reimagine meaningful gospel conversations? Our work here necessitates that we consider how we might engage in a meaningful gospel conversation with persons like Ariana.

The Universe Has Your Back

I have also noticed an increasing number of references to "the universe" in pop culture, media, and general conversation. The universe is referred to as an animate, all-knowing, all-wise entity to which we look for guidance, meaning, and protection. Increasingly, people look to the universe to manifest their destiny, to validate relationship or career choices, to verify the coincidental, or to discover their true purpose. What or who is the universe?

As I began to research this phenomenon, I discovered a mystical world of belief, filled with mindfulness, motivation, and self-help. Social media influencer Gabrielle Bernstein caught my attention right away. She's numbered among Oprah's Super Soul 100—a handpicked group of innovators, trailblazers, and visionaries who purpose together to move humanity forward. Gabby Bernstein embodies an accessible modern-day spiritual movement that transforms lives through her podcast, books, and conferences.

Bernstein's journey to fulfillment began at a point of crisis that prompted her to immerse herself in spiritual principles and meditation practices. This process, she claims, helped her to discover her true purpose, to love and inspire the world. Her stated mission is "to lead others to their highest potential," and her goal is "to help you manifest your dreams and live with more peace and joy than you ever thought possible."[9] She promises her followers the pathway

---

[9] Gabby Bernstein, "Meet Gabby: Your Presence is Your Power," accessed August 1, 2023, https://gabbybernstein.com/about-gabby/.

to manifesting a life beyond their wildest dreams and provides live online meditation and coaching, a monthly mantra as the pathway to enduring happiness, anxiety relief, and much more.

In a post titled, "How to Trust the Universe,"[10] Bernstein describes the universe as an infinite force of love that surrounds everything. One of her stated goals is to help people establish a spiritual relationship with a higher power of their own understanding, one that makes sense to them. Bernstein, in her book *The Universe Has Your Back: Transform Fear to Faith,* invites her audience to connect with and pray to the universe. "I call on the energy of the Universe to guide my thoughts back to love. I surrender the false perceptions I have placed upon myself. I forgive these thoughts and I know that I am love. I am peace. I am compassion. I am the Universe."[11]

These cultural fables illustrate Taylor's understanding of secularization. They embody exclusive humanism in different ways, providing examples of appealing counternarratives, caricatures of truth. For Grande, God is a woman, and for Bernstein, we are the universe and masters of our own destiny. I highlight these to urge us to embrace the fact that our cultural context is no longer predominantly Christian. I also hope to alert us to the fact that these narratives both run counter to the True Story. Our context today is secularized—our assumptions about morality, identity, and history, or our traditional beliefs about religion and God, identity, and purpose are constantly in flux. What insight does the True Story provide in instances like this one? How might we engage in a conversation with Ariana or Gabby?

[10] Gabby Bernstein, "How to Trust the Universe," accessed August 1, 2023, https://gabbybernstein.com/how-to-trust-the-universe/.

[11] Gabby Bernstein, *The Universe Has Your Back: Transform Fear to Faith* (Carlsbad, CA: Hay House, 2016), 148.

Reflection

I started this chapter by describing various ways that my ordered understanding of God and the gospel was being sifted and sorted through my research, reading, and re-reading of the Bible. I highlighted the True Story as the metanarrative of Scripture—four key themes and six acts that pulsate across the storyline. These themes and acts provide balance and perspective in our secularized context. They provide the necessary components of a *missional framework* and the building blocks for a narrative approach to meaningful gospel conversations. Before we discuss a missional framework, let us return to Cru's research and some significant findings.

CHAPTER 4

From Presentation to Conversation

This book began with my encounter with a college freshman who was willing to take our religious survey. When we asked her the very first question, "Who, in your opinion, is Jesus Christ?" she answered, "I have no idea what you're talking about." In fact, she had no context for God, the Bible, or church. The journey that began for me on that fall day continues still today, as I observe and experience the reverberating effects of the changing culture. Even though my research began nearly a decade ago, I continue to engage with all kinds of people who embody the secularization I introduced in chapter 2.

For example, I had an interesting conversation today just before I started working on this chapter. I am a member of a shared work-space in my city where I spend several days a week writing and preparing presentations. I enjoy the shared space and the opportunities to meet new people. Today, a young woman introduced herself to me, explaining that she moved to the United States from India about six years ago to earn a master's degree and, most recently, a PhD.

I, in turn, told her that I work for a faith-based nonprofit organization as a writer and speaker and that I have a PhD as well. She was excited to tell me that she attends a weekly Bible study online with some friends she met when she was in grad school. When I asked what they were studying, she replied, "Well, I'm new to the Bible. I am a Hindu but believe in God and all gods." Now, from a missiological and contextual perspective, it is important to know that the suburb where I live is reportedly 42 percent South Asian, nearly double what it was a decade ago. Many of the South Asians (Indians) I meet in my neighborhood are devoted Hindus and very open to discussing spirituality, gods, and God. In fact, several friends who happen to be Hindus attend a regular prayer time at our neighborhood gazebo.

Until just a few years ago, I had never met a Hindu and knew next to nothing about Hinduism. I am still learning, but I know enough to understand how it is possible for my new friend to attend a Bible study, remain a devoted Hindu, and believe that Jesus is not unlike deities in the Hindu framework. A meaningful gospel conversation with a Hindu requires a new set of skills and a firm belief that God is the One who reveals the truth of the gospel. So, like many of you, I am learning how to engage in a variety of conversations that I hope will develop into friendships and even provoke a deeper look at the God of the Bible.

Importantly, this experience and so many others have caused me to make an adjustment to my ongoing research question, from "How can Cru train others to present the gospel in a twenty-first-century American context and honor Bill Bright's vision and maintain his commitment to evangelism?"[1] to "How can we train Christians to be gospel witnesses in a twenty-first-century American context, and to eagerly make Jesus known?" Fortunately, I am not alone. I find that many churches and Christian organizations are wrestling with the question of relevance in today's context.

We discovered in chapter 1 that Bill Bright was deliberate in his efforts to understand his mid-century context. He followed in

---

[1]   Monaco, "Bill Bright's," xv (see chap. 1, n. 1).

Henrietta Mears's entrepreneurial footsteps and aggressively surveyed thousands of college students to determine their religious beliefs and backgrounds. The most compelling finding for Bright was the fact that most people were familiar with the God of the Bible and understood that Jesus died to pay for humankind's sin. However, many had no idea that they could have a personal relationship with God. As noted in chapter 1, *Four Spiritual Laws* became one of the most widely used gospel tracts in personal evangelism and provided the basis for all kinds of innovative approaches for answering the prevailing question of the day, "Is it true?"

In chapter 2, I introduced four missiological snapshots that help us to understand today's secularized context from four different vantage points: (1) Introducing Secularization, (2) Cru's Research, (3) Demographics and a Diversity Explosion, and (4) Gen Z, the Next Generation. I contend that the US context is best described as secularized. In today's era, people find belief in God implausible, even unimaginable. I compared this assertion with Bill Bright's context in the mid-twentieth century. Remember, and I restate these statistics again for emphasis, according to Gallup, in the 1950s over half of the Americans surveyed identified as Protestant, 24 percent as Catholic, and 4 percent as Jewish. Most of the evangelism tools and training employed today originated in this religious context.

I also pointed out that most people today, unlike any generation before, view the world based entirely on what they can explain or experience without any reference to God. This denial of the supernatural has led to what Canadian philosopher Charles Taylor describes as *exclusive humanism*—a radical new option in the marketplace of beliefs—loyal only to this present existence, with no final goal beyond human flourishing. Importantly, Taylor's secularization is not void of spirituality, but is loaded with beliefs. This "galloping pluralism on the spiritual plane" treats Christianity as one option among an explosion of others.[2] A prevailing question I often hear in today's context is "Who is Jesus and why does he matter?"

As discussed in chapter 3, understanding the True Story opens a new vista for understanding the gospel and having meaningful gospel conversations. First, the True Story reminds us that the Bible is full of people who encounter God through his witnesses, often in unconventional ways. Second, the True Story gives us bearings amid the shifts I described earlier. Third, a continuous reading of the True Story—from Genesis to Revelation—helps us to develop a greater awareness of the people around us. Neighbors, pharmacists, baristas, dentists, classmates, grandpas, and aunties are more than objects for my presentation but are instead living, breathing human beings on a journey with a story to tell.

In this chapter, first, I return to Cru's research and reveal another significant finding related to our audience. Second, I introduce three pathways for meaningful gospel conversations that emerged from the research and are relevant in our secularized context: three core longings, three-statement stories, and five behavior changes (see chap. 2, n. 5).

Cru's Research Revisited

By way of reminder, Cru's research project, "Understanding Faith and Purpose in the City," surveyed 400 men and women across the United States representing various ethnicities, ages, backgrounds, and worldviews. Significantly, of those surveyed, over half claimed no religious affiliation and most found Christianity either offensive, inauthentic, irrelevant, or unsafe.[3] Not only was Christianity just one

---

[2]   Taylor, *A Secular Age*, 300 (see chap. 2, n. 5).

[3]   Wright et al., "Understanding Faith" (see chap. 2, n. 1).

option among a myriad of others, but it was also among the least appealing.

Let that sink in for a few minutes. "Over half of the people surveyed found Christianity either offensive, inauthentic, irrelevant, or unsafe." Such a sobering realization. But at least our research validated our experience and gave shape to this idea of secularization. As a scale of belief emerged from the data, we realized that we needed to accept the fact that most people don't share the same faith we do today, and most happily believe something very different from us. In fact, many people today are perfectly content—they don't believe in God and don't even think about God.

Importantly, for devoted followers of Jesus, these realizations can feel disorienting and might even cause us to question our beliefs. This disorientation is consistent with Charles Taylor's secularization. He describes this phenomenon as being "fragilized." Suddenly, due to these "cross-pressures," we are caught between our own beliefs and the myriad beliefs around us, and *we* experience uncertainty.

But imagine this: 84 percent of those surveyed indicated a willingness to engage in conversations with Christians. We celebrated—this is GREAT NEWS. However, and strikingly, those surveyed also believe that Christians are unwilling and unprepared to participate in a conversation with someone who holds an opposing point of view. This compelled us to dig a little deeper to understand how to better engage with the people around us, which resulted in the three core longings and the five behavior changes.

Pathways for Meaningful Gospel Conversations

In chapter 3 we considered four prominent themes found in the True Story: Creation, Rebellion, Redemption, and New Creation. God's creation of Adam and Eve—the first human beings—is his crowning act. We learn right away that God created humankind in God's own image or likeness: "So God created man in his own image; he created him in the image of God; he created them male and female." (Gen 1:27).

This mind-bending truth means that in some fundamental way we are like God. How exactly? We learn in Gen 1:26 that God created humankind for a purpose: "Then God said, 'Let us make man in our image, according to our likeness. They will rule the fish of the sea, the birds of the sky, the livestock, the whole earth, and the creatures that crawl on the earth.'" Just as God rules as our King, we are to be like God in the exercise of our responsibilities. Consider the fact that God creates humans with a conscious rationality and with bodies that have the capacity to cultivate the earth to produce food necessary to eat.

God also created us for the purpose of relationship—with each other, with ourselves, with the created world, and most importantly with God. God made us for himself. Craig Bartholomew and Paige Vanosky put it this way, "We are made to love and to be loved, and as we are loved and love, we become fully alive."[4] As we mined the research, we discovered that we are all hardwired by God with three core longings (See Figure 4).

---

[4] Craig G. Bartholomew and Paige P. Vanosky, *The 30-Minute Bible: God's Story for Everyone* (Downers Grove: IVP, 2021), 21.

Three Core Longings:

Figure 4. Infographic of Three Core Longings. Brooke Wright et al. *Understanding Faith and Purpose in the City*. Atlanta: Cyrano Marketing

The Imago Dei: Three Core Longings

The first core longing we discovered is peace—the absence of anxiety. Most of us long for well-being and a peaceful existence. We look forward to restful weekends, we strive to resolve conflict, we work hard to eliminate anxiety and to assuage our worried minds. On the global front, we look to governments to bring an end to war, and we form alliances and write treaties with the goal of peace between borders. The True Story is replete with loud cries of lament and longing for peace during catastrophe and evidence of how it is the longing for peace that brings us to God.

The second core longing is prosperity—the shared longing for security. For some, the idea of prosperity means financial wealth, but the Bible helps us to see that prosperity is something much deeper; it is a longing for security—a safe place to live, enough food to feed the family, and enough money to pay the bills. Today we witness this longing for prosperity at a global level as people of nearly every age, desperate for a sense of security, migrate thousands of miles to reach the safe-haven in places like the United States and Canada, the United Kingdom, Europe, and Ethiopia. The COVID-19 pandemic demonstrates the lengths we will go to ensure safety and security.

The third core longing is purpose—the deep longing to make a difference. People the world over ask the question, "Why am I here?" and "What is my purpose?" Often, people are unaware of their Creator and have no idea that God created all of us for relation-ship, to work, to multiply and fill the earth, and to cultivate the land. Our research revealed that people from all walks of life long to make a difference in this life and want to contribute to something bigger than themselves.

**Peace:
What we
long for**

**Prosperity:
What we
care about**

**Purpose:
Why we are
here**

Figure 5. Infographic of Three Core Longings. Brooke Wright et al. *Understanding Faith and Purpose in the City*. Atlanta: Cyrano Marketing

These descriptions of peace, prosperity, and purpose are not exhaus-tive but shed light on our shared longings and often lead to mean-ingful gospel conversations. Importantly, the easiest way to engage in conversation is from the outside of the circle in. For most of us, identifying our longing for peace or the things we care about is easy. Conversely, discussing our purpose, or answering existential questions related to our purpose, often takes place after trust is developed, because our purpose or motivation is personal and more intimate. Sometimes, we are invited to contribute or to share our experiences, and ultimately, we learn together as we share common longings and experiences.

Five Behavior Changes

Earlier, I mentioned that 84 percent of the 400 people we surveyed indicated a willingness to engage in spiritual conversations with Christians, but many of those surveyed also believed that Christians are unwilling and unprepared to engage in conversations with people who hold a different point of view. Suddenly, the research pointed back to us as believers—something needed to change in us! As we considered the data, we discovered five behavior changes that we believe will help us to cultivate meaningful conversations.

(1) Be present and listen—follow the conversation and not your agenda. Basically, learn to listen closely and ask reflective questions. Yes, this is Communication 101. But for those of us trained to make a gospel presentation it is essential that we learn to be present and listen. One of the ways I try to be present is by keeping my phone in my purse to avoid the inevitable distraction. Another way is that I try to restate what I am hearing to make sure I understand.

I often pray before I spend time with someone—for wisdom and compassion and for the grace to follow the Spirit who guides the conversation. Jesus, just after feeding 5,000 people, reminds his audience, "No one can come to me unless the Father who sent me draws him" (John 6:44). My friend Juerg Schaufelberger prays this prayer, "Father, show me, who have you prepared to know You today'?"

(2) Find common ground—build a relational bridge. Often, in our neighborhoods or at work, and even in our families, we encounter

people who are different from us, who are antagonistic toward God, or who are wary of people asking questions. Nevertheless, I find that most people are willing to share some basic information about themselves to begin with and often, if the conversation continues, we find common ground. For instance, during a recent trip to Manhattan, I took an Uber from my hotel to the meeting I was attending. I asked the driver how long he had been driving and if business had improved since COVID-19 restrictions had been lifted (by the way, we all have COVID-19 in common).

He readily shared that he had been a taxi driver since the September 11, 2001, terrorist attacks. He told me something of his experience back then and, more recently, during the worst of the COVID-19 hospitalizations in New York City. He described a grim reality of life during those dark days and how driving gave him a sense of purpose. We had a meaningful conversation in his car that morning, and I thanked him for being an "essential worker."

(3) Walk in their shoes—understand their story. This might mean sitting with someone in their grief, or it might mean saying nothing at all. The conversations I had with Isa on my way to Orlando and the two students I mentioned in the last chapter are good examples of what can happen when we change our posture. This behavior change has been significant for me and requires an attentiveness, a willingness to learn, and patience to understand a person's lack of interest or another's hostility.

(4) Talk like a real person—use words meant for people, not for the pews. For me, this hasn't meant I don't talk about God—I do, but I try to use words that help to make sense of God, or prayer, or faith. For example, I often pray for my friends who don't yet know Jesus when they face challenging health issues or when they are anxious about work or family, just like I pray for my husband or my niece or myself. At the same time, I am aware that prayer has

been trivialized in our culture. So, to personalize and legitimatize #Praying and #Blessing, I explain what I mean by praying—that I am talking with and asking the God who created us for help or healing or comfort. I also encourage them to pray and call on God for help or peace.

(5) Tell a better story than the one they have heard by connecting their story to the True Story. Often, after standing in someone's shoes, we realize that, possibly, the story they have heard about Christianity is skewed by a bad experience or distorted by misinformation. In these cases, we can "tell a better story" by responding to skepticism or lack of trust with understanding or by sharing from our personal experience. Jesus knows pain and sorrow, and he understands betrayal and injustice. In the same way that Jesus and the gospel transformed us, he also brings redemption to our story and adds a whole new chapter.

Three-Statement Stories
These discoveries continue to radically change my conversations, and today I have quite a few friends who do not know Jesus yet, but they know I do. In some situations, I've been able to share openly about personal challenges, like my ten-year bout with a chronic virus or our long journey related to infertility. In other situations, I am available to commiserate with people who are agonizing over the challenges of graduate school and PhD research. More recently, I meet people who, like me, lost loved ones during COVID-19 and need a place to process their grief. I am discovering that it is a lot easier to live my faith out loud, so-to-speak, than to minimize my relationship with God for fear that I will be misunderstood or might offend someone.

We live in an era of heightened anxiety and fear, and we can be conduits for the gospel of God by simply telling people how he meets us in places of anxiety, insecurity, and meaninglessness. My friend and colleague, Gary Runn, in response to these three core longings, developed a "Three-Statement Story" that helps us to personally process our anxieties and needs and our longing for peace and hope.[5] When we take time to answer these questions ourselves, we are often better prepared to enter an authentic conversation. As I previously disclosed, people today are no longer asking "Did Jesus exist?" but, instead, "Who is Jesus," and "Why does Jesus matter?" These real-time testimonies help to demonstrate why Jesus matters to us and the difference it makes to know God. Here are three questions that help us form three personal statements.

- Where are you experiencing some level of anxiety right now?
- How is God meeting you at your point of need?
- How is this bringing you peace and hope for the future?

Notably, I have found that these appear to be simple questions for us as followers of Jesus to answer. On the one hand, for many of us, these questions take time and thought to answer, and on the other hand, answering these questions honestly in the presence of other believers feels scary, maybe even threatening, to us. While I am curious as to how we got here, I am increasingly convinced that engaging in significant conversations about God and the gospel *with each other* prepares us to converse with others along the way.

I stated at the beginning of this chapter that Cru's research revealed that of the 400 men and women surveyed, over half claimed no religious affiliation, and most found Christianity either offensive,

---

[5]   Cas Monaco and Gary Runn, "Scattering Gospel Seeds: Moments and Conversations," Wheaton Billy Graham Center, July 16, 2018, accessed December 19, 2022, https://wheatonbillygraham.com/scattering-gospel-seeds/.

inauthentic, irrelevant, or unsafe.[6] Not only was Christianity just one option among a myriad of others, but it was also among the least appealing.

We realized we need to accept the fact that most people do not share the same faith we do today. Some happily believe something altogether different, and a fair number of people do not care or even think about God. What caught our attention was the 84 percent who indicated a willingness to engage in spiritual conversations with Christians. This was coupled with their belief that Christians are unwilling and unprepared to engage in conversations with people who hold a different point of view. These findings validated our experience and compelled us to lean in a little closer in order to understand a little better. Along the way, three core longings, five behavior changes, and three-statement stories emerged. These results apply as much to us as believers as they do to the 84 percent in our survey.

Reflection

I spent ten days with my dad in Billings, Montana, in the summer of 2018. He was recovering from life-threatening complications of femoral bypass surgery, and I had volunteered to help him while he convalesced in a long-term recovery center. From there, I flew to Atlanta for some meetings before going home. From the airport, I took an Uber to the hotel where I'd spend the next few nights. The friendly Uber driver had a cross on a chain hanging from his rear-view mirror, so I asked, "I'm a follower of Jesus; are you too?" He replied, "Yes, I am!"

---

6   Wright et al., "Understanding Faith."

As the conversation started, we shared the usual details about life and work, and I ended up telling him about my dad, his poor health, and his lack of interest in God and the gospel. I explained how I'd prayed for my dad for nearly forty years, and still, after all this time, he remained indifferent. The driver proceeded to tell me about his two older brothers who had both lived very hard lives into middle age, and one had even spent time in prison. Even though neither of them had any interest in God, the driver and his family kept praying. Eventually, both brothers, at the very end of their lives on earth, placed their faith in Jesus.

The driver exhorted and encouraged me to not lose heart. God is faithful no matter what. This stranger, a brother, connected his story, my story, and my dad's story to the True Story. When we arrived at the hotel, we stopped and prayed together and expressed joy in our common bond in Jesus Christ. My point here is that there is almost always a way to connect our story or someone else's to the True Story, and sometimes when we are the ones who need encouragement, the Spirit of God sends someone across our paths to minister to us.

Men and women of all ages long to have someone to talk to. Surprisingly, the more we pay attention and listen, the more often we find that people are willing to share their story. Sometimes, they want to hear ours as well. As we make the shift from making a presentation to having a conversation, we are freed up to share about the reality of our relationship with God, which sometimes includes the experience of God's love, comfort, and peace, while other times includes doubts, frustrations, and confusion. The kind of meaningful conversations I am talking about require something more of us today, including a willingness to engage with people on a deeper, more emotional level. The next chapter introduces a missional framework that seeks to provide some theological handrails and riverbanks for meaningful gospel engagement in a secular age.

CHAPTER 5

Introducing a Missional Framework

I n the fall of 2022, I had the privilege of attending a conference in Latin America sponsored by FamilyLife® (a ministry of Cru). It was the first FamilyLife® gathering of its kind. Over 300 people attended, representing seventeen different countries in Latin America, most of whom serve as FamilyLife® volunteers in various cities. The excitement and depth of commitment I observed and experienced is hard to capture in words.

The conference included a variety of workshops, including mine on "Gospel Conversations Reimagined: A Reverse Workshop." Since my research targeted a twenty-first-century American context, I knew that my findings and conclusions might not exactly fit the wide array of countries represented. So, I created a "reverse workshop" to encourage an environment of mutual learning and collaboration between people from places like Jamaica, the United States, Colombia, Peru, Ecuador, Panama, and El Salvador.

I introduced my research methodology and findings and engaged the group by using Cru's "Soularium," a set of fifty original photographic images that serve to prompt personal reflection and encourage group interaction.[1] In this workshop, I asked participants

---

[1] Cru, "Soularium," accessed December 28, 2022, https://www.cru.org/us/en /train-and-grow/share-the-gospel/outreach-strategies/soularium/soularium-overview. html. Soularium is also available for free from the App Store and Google Play.

to choose an image that best describes their experience coming out of the COVID-19 pandemic—an experience we have all shared across the world. I also asked them to be prepared to share the Soularium image they chose and to explain why it represents their experience coming out of COVID-19. Their lively conversations revealed the significance of this shared experience.

Then, I presented my research findings, much like I have so far in this book, and provided time for small group interaction around two or three related questions. Primarily, I asked them to discuss how my findings are similar to or different from their context and to determine what steps they might take to better understand people in their part of Latin America. I concluded the discussion by high-lighting the fact that many people in our spheres of influence experienced isolation, anxiety, frustration, and loss just like us. Using the Soularium process is one way we can enter into meaningful gospel conversations with people all around us.

After the first session, a participant named Chris told me how my findings related to his campus ministry context in Colombia. He referenced the Global Youth Culture and reminded me that we all have so much in common due to the influence of mass media, global economics, and the internet.[2] The phrase Global Youth Culture was vaguely familiar to me, and the more we talked the more intrigued I became.

At the same time, I began to get to know Laura, my Colombian translator. She is a recent college graduate and is currently

---

[2] Richard Kahn and Douglas Kellner, in "Global Youth Culture," UCLA, August 29, 2006, accessed January 11, 2023, define Global Youth Culture as "the transdisciplinary category by which theorists and policy analysts attempt to understand the emergence of the complex forms of hybrid culture and identity that increasingly occur amongst youth throughout the world due to the proliferation of media like film, television, popular music, the Internet, and other information and communication technologies (ICTs) in their everyday lives."

involved with an international organization called Steiger. In fact, it was through Steiger that she and a group of her friends were tasked to serve at this conference. She explained that Steiger began in Amsterdam in 1983 at the height of the European punk rock movement through the ministry of David and Jodi Pierce. They started a Bible study back then on a barge known as "Steiger 14" behind the Central Train Station to reach the city's punks and anarchists.

Today, Steiger International is active in over 100 cities around the globe. Steiger missionaries have been sharing the gospel along the margins for a long time. Now, through their experience and expertise, we can learn a lot about how to engage global youth and how to engage with a secularized culture. Not surprisingly, their approach to sharing the gospel springs from questions like "Who am I?" "Why am I here?" and "What is my purpose?" These questions correspond with my findings introduced in chapter 2 and the *imago Dei* and the three core longings introduced in chapter 4.

This encounter with Chris, Laura, and other FamilyLife® volunteers in Latin America validated much of my research and fueled my passion to answer the question I posed in chapter 1 and reframed in chapter 4, "How can we train Christians to be gospel witnesses in a twenty-first-century American context, and to eagerly make Jesus known?"

I introduce a missional framework in this chapter that builds upon the True Story. Here I contend that a robust theological missiology reinforces the fact that God empowers us as witnesses in today's secularized context for at least three reasons. First, it provides us with an interpretive guide or hermeneutic for understanding the storyline of Scripture. Second, it serves as a blueprint for the mission of God, the *missio Dei*, and invites us to participate with God as vibrant witnesses. Third, it serves as a framework that shapes our worldview—how we express our deepest, most basic understanding of reality. I conclude this chapter by glancing back at Bill Bright's emphasis on the Great Commission and demonstrate how a missional hermeneutic reframes and enriches our understanding of the Great Commission as it resounds across the canon of Scripture. A missional framework sets the stage for what I describe as "a reimagined approach to meaningful gospel conversations grounded in the biblical narrative" and is explained in chapter 6.[3]

What is a "Missional Framework"?

When I started seminary, I thought I was familiar with the Bible—after all, I had been reading and studying it for a very long time. In fact, I was fortunate to meet men and women early in my faith journey who encouraged me to get to know God by reading the Bible and to "master the Bible one book at a time." So, for decades I had approached my Bible reading and study with that goal in mind. I had studied numerous books in both the OT and NT. I frequently turned to the Bible to learn more about God and my salvation and specifically to the Psalms and Proverbs when I was in search of peace or guidance.

But I never fully appreciated the fact that the entire biblical narrative tells the story of the *missio Dei* and provides a historically grounded and meaningful account of universal human history. As I began to read the Bible through the lens of the True Story, my understanding of the *missio Dei* began to grow. I realized in a whole new way that the triune God, the hero of the Bible, is a missionary God who makes his name known and invites ordinary and even unlikely people like us everywhere to participate in the *missio Dei.*

---

[3]   Monaco, "Bill Bright's" 189 (see chap. 1, n. 1).

Developing a Missional Hermeneutic

Developing a missional hermeneutic helps to guide our interpretation of Scripture through the lens of the *missio Dei,* a lens that focuses on God's mission as its central interest and goal. A missional hermeneutic is trinitarian and Christ-centered (or *Christocentric*), rests on the full weight of God's authority, and mirrors the diverse, multicultural and multiethnic reality of the twenty-first century.

Trinitarian

A trinitarian understanding of God and the *missio Dei*, a key component of a missional framework, includes an affirmation that the triune God—Father, Son, and Spirit—redeems and restores every dimension of creation. The Trinity acts together as one. Consider God's fatherly rule over all things—the heart of the Bible's message. He sustains, loves, and cares for all. God the Son, Jesus, acknowledges God the Father as the spokesperson whose voice he loves, hears, and obeys. In turn, Jesus has been sent to make the Father's name known:

> O righteous Father, even though the world does not know
> you, I know you, and these know that you have sent me.
> I made known to them your name, and I will continue to
> make it known, that the love with which you have loved
> me may be in them, and I in them. (John 17:25–26 ESV)

God the Spirit makes the Son known and, in turn, also makes the Father known. Furthermore, God's Spirit shines a light on or illumines God's Word and gives us the ability to comprehend God and God's love for us. Importantly, the Spirit leads, empowers, guides, and prompts us to participate in the *missio Dei* (John 14:24–25; 16:12–13).

A missional hermeneutic also emphasizes a trinitarian under-standing of redemption that highlights the community of the Trinity. God the Father created all things through the Son and sent the Son to redeem all things. Jesus Christ accomplished redemption through his incarnation, crucifixion, and resurrection. Jesus Christ makes all things new and now and forever rules over all of creation (Matt 28:18; John 1:1–4, 14; Rom 1:1–7; 5:1–7; 8:18–30; Col 1:15–22; Heb 1:1–4; Rev 19:11–18; 21:1–8). The Spirit of God is sent by the Father and the Son to lead and empower the church to be God's witnesses for the sake of the whole creation. In fact, I argue that the book of Acts, traditionally understood as the "Acts of the Apos-tles," is more accurately described as the "Acts of the Holy Spirit," who works to spread the gospel from the first century to the twenty-first century. The Spirit empowers the church as a community of believers to build relationships of mutuality and trust and invites the church to participate in the *missio Dei* as God's signpost in the world.

CHRISTOCENTRIC

A missional hermeneutic is Christocentric. Jesus Christ, the Son of God and Son of Man, situated in a specific time and place in history, is the plumb line for human history and the *missio Dei*. First, at the center of God's mission is the *incarnation*—God became flesh in the power of the Holy Spirit (John 1:14–18). This emphasis on the incarnation by no means minimizes the crucifixion but intensifies the self-giving of God on our behalf. Jesus, the incarnate Son of God, took on human flesh and helps us to understand God and his love for the world. He models for us how to enter and engage with local culture—whoever we are and wherever we live. We discover that, in Christ, the good news of God's kingdom extends to every tribe, tongue, and nation.

Second, Jesus also taught his disciples that the one who will reign as king must first suffer unto death. Jesus, during the last few years of his life, encountered unbelief, constant scrutiny, false accusations, and eventual condemnation. Jesus, as both the Son of God and the Son of Man, paid the ultimate price for humankind's rebellion through the *crucifixion*. Isaiah's Suffering Servant, sent by Yahweh to suffer and bear the iniquities of many, experienced rejection, injustice, and, eventually, brutal death. In an astounding way, he was vindicated and exalted. In fact, Jesus Christ fulfilled Isaiah's prophecies (Isa 42:1–9; 49:1–6; 50:2–9; 52:13–53:12). The writer of Hebrews sheds light on the comprehensive nature of Christ's life and death:

> Now since the children have flesh and blood in common, Jesus also shared in these, so that through his death he might destroy the one holding the power of death—that is, the devil—and free those who were held in slavery all their lives by the fear of death. For it is clear that he does not reach out to help angels, but to help Abraham's offspring.

> Therefore, he had to be like his brothers and sisters in every way, so that he could become a merciful and faithful high priest in matters pertaining to God, to make atonement for the sins of the people. For since he himself has suffered when he was tempted, he is able to help those who are tempted. (Heb 2:14–18)

Third, Jesus was raised from the dead by the power of the Spirit (Rom 1:4; 8:11–13; 1 Pet 3:18) and through the *resurrection* we celebrate God's victory over wickedness, violence, torture, and sin.

Jesus Christ is the firstborn of the new creation, and through the resurrection, new life in Christ is possible.

> He is the image of the invisible God, the firstborn over all
> creation. For everything was created by him, in heaven
> and on earth, the visible and the invisible, whether thrones
> or dominions or rulers or authorities—all things have been
> created through him and for him. He is before all things,
> and by him all things hold together. He is also the head
> of the body, the church; he is the beginning, the firstborn
> from the dead, so that he might come to have first place in
> everything. For God was pleased to have all his fullness
> dwell in him, and through him to reconcile everything to
> himself, whether things on earth or things in heaven, by
> making peace through his blood, shed on the cross. (Col
> 1:15–20)

The Full Weight of God's Authority

So, our missional hermeneutic is both trinitarian and Christocentric and is also grounded in the full weight of God's authority. God is the Creator and Sustainer of all things, beginning with the creation of the entire universe and culminating in the new creation. Importantly, by acknowledging God as the Creator and Sustainer of all things, we affirm that God continues to be active in and has all authority over creation all the time. Yes, God created the heavens, the earth, and humankind "in the beginning," but our missional hermeneutic reveals that the True Story emphasizes God's continuing authority over all creation for all time (Genesis 1–3; Num 14:21; Deut 4:36–39; Pss 45:5–7; 90; 95; 103:19; Jer 31:35–37; Hab 2:14; 2 Cor 4:6).

Space does not allow me to recount all the ways that the Creator shows up in the Scripture and in our lives, but let me assure you, the Creator is present in every act of the True Story. We see the Creator at work in the lives of Abraham and Sarah when God promises to make Abraham the father of many nations—even though Sarah was barren. Then, twenty-five long years later, when Abraham and Sarah considered themselves already dead, God blesses them with a son (Gen 17:15–21; 21:1–7; Rom 4:18–19).

The Creator is actively involved in Israel's deliverance from Egypt and demonstrates in awesome and sometimes terrifying ways that God's authority continues to be active over life and death, disease and famine, locusts and livestock, and the land and sea. Later, in the book of Numbers, God speaks to Balaam through the mouth of a donkey. In the book of Judges, he gives Samson superhuman strength determined by the length of his hair. And in 1 Kings, he provides a bountiful supply of oil for a widow and her sons to pay off their debts. The psalmists retell these stories and remind us,

> The LORD is a great God,
> a great King above all gods.
> The depths of the earth are in his hand,
> and the mountain peaks are his.
> The sea is his; he made it.
> His hands formed the dry land.
> Come, let's worship and bow down;
> let's kneel before the LORD our Maker.
> For he is our God,
> and we are the people of his pasture,
> the sheep under his care. (Ps 95:3–7)

In the NT we meet Mary, a teenager, and a virgin, who is betrothed to Joseph. She miraculously conceives by the life-giving work of the Holy Spirit and gives birth to the Son of God. This logic-defying event sets into motion awesome displays of the Creator's power and authority over creation. Later, Jesus displays authority over Satan's temptations in the wilderness, turns water into wine, calms the wind and the sea, raises the dead to life, heals the lame, gives sight to the blind, and eludes the grasp of his enemies time and again.

God's authority over all things is evidenced by the fulfillment of OT prophecies made manifest in Jesus. For example, in Matthew 4:13–17, we find Jesus reading from the prophet Isaiah and announcing the arrival of God's kingdom:

> He left Nazareth and went to live in Capernaum by the sea, in the region of Zebulun and Naphtali. This was to fulfill what was spoken through the prophet Isaiah:
> **Land of Zebulun and land of Naphtali,**
> **along the road by the sea, beyond the Jordan,**
> **Galilee of the Gentiles.**
> **The people who live in darkness**
> **have seen a great light,**
> **and for those living in the land of the shadow of death,**
> **a light has dawned.**
> From then on Jesus began to preach, "Repent, because the kingdom of heaven has come near." (Matt 4:13–17)

We can look back to Daniel's vision of the Son of Man who reigns in glory over an indestructible kingdom where all peoples, nations, and languages serve him (Dan 7:13–14). Likewise, God, through Jeremiah, points to a new era when "they will be my people, and I will be their God. I will give them integrity of heart and action so that they will fear me always" (Jer 32:38–39). The writer of Hebrews opens in worship, rejoicing that God's promise is fulfilled in Christ—the King who reigns with redemptive power (Jer 32:38–40; Heb 1:1–3; 8:8–12).

Jesus personally continues to reign as King over all of creation, and we now look forward with great hope to his second coming and the new creation, God's kingdom that is yet to come (Revelation 19–21). We rest in God's promise repeated throughout the narrative,

> For the earth will be filled
> with the knowledge of the LORD's glory,
> as the water covers the sea. (Hab 2:14)

Until that day, we serve God as faithful witnesses:

> For we are not proclaiming ourselves but Jesus Christ
> as Lord, and ourselves as your servants for Jesus's sake.
> For God who said, "Let light shine out of darkness," has
> shone in our hearts to give the light of the knowledge of
> God's glory in the face of Jesus Christ. (2 Cor 4:5–6)

Multicultural and Multiethnic Contexts

Faithful recontextualization that reflects the multiethnic, multicultural reality of today's context includes at least three components. First, it necessarily draws from the True Story and yields to the full weight of God's authority. Second, it requires a heightened awareness of the surrounding cultural and societal variation and collaborates intra- and cross-culturally. Third, it taps into the priesthood of *all* believers from every nation (1 Pet 2:4–10; Rev 5:9–10).

Blueprint for the *Missio Dei*

In the previous section, I introduced a missional hermeneutic that is: (1) trinitarian; (2) Christocentric; (3) yields to the full weight of God's authority; and (4) reflects the multicultural reality of our twenty-first century context. Our missiological framework introduces us to the True Story, played out in six acts, briefly discussed in chapter 3.

The Bible provides a blueprint for the *missio Dei* that stretches back to Adam and Eve and is recognized again in Noah's encounter with the Lord. God, grieved by man's violence and wickedness, decides to blot out every living thing on the face of the earth. However, Noah found favor in God's eyes and was chosen to build an ark to deliver his family and all kinds of animals from a catastrophic flood. God displays his holiness and judgment and shows mercy by redeeming and delivering Noah and his passengers from the flood. God promises to never again curse the ground, marking his covenant with Noah and all of humanity, by a rainbow (Gen 8:21; 9:12-17).

Then, God commissions Noah, his family, and every living thing to be fruitful and multiply and to fill the earth just as he had commissioned Adam and Eve (Gen 1:28; 8:17; 9:1, 7). In the chapters that follow, the nations of the world emerge through Noah's sons and their offspring and they, too, rebel against God, evidenced in part by the Tower of Babel (Genesis 10–11). However, God remains steadfast, and, in Genesis 12, he calls Abraham to leave his family and his country to receive God's blessing:

> The LORD said to Abram:
> Go from your land,
> your relatives,
> and your father's house

to the land that I will show you.
I will make you into a great nation,
I will bless you,
I will make your name great,
and you will be a blessing.
I will bless those who bless you,
I will curse anyone who treats you with contempt,
and all the peoples on earth
will be blessed through you. (Gen 12:1–3)

God blesses Abraham and promises to bless all the peoples of the earth through him, and eventually, through his grandson Jacob, the nation of Israel is born.

The book of Exodus declares, "But the Israelites were fruitful, increased rapidly, multiplied, and became extremely numerous so that the land was filled with them" (Exod 1:7). But by this time, God's people labor under the oppressive rule of Pharoah. So, God calls Moses to deliver Israel from the land of Egypt and into the Promised Land, where he restates his promise to Israel and makes a covenant with them (Exodus 19, 24).

This is what you must say to the house of Jacob and explain to the Israelites: "You have seen what I did to the Egyptians and how I carried you on eagles' wings and brought you to myself. Now if you will carefully listen to me and keep my covenant, you will be my own possession out of all the peoples, although the whole earth is mine, and you will be my kingdom of priests and my holy nation." These are the words that you are to say to the Israelites. (Exod 19:3–6)

Later, God establishes his covenant with David, the prince over Israel, and promises to raise up a king from David's offspring and to provide a place for God's people to dwell in peace. This is fulfilled in Jesus Christ, the Son of David (1 Chron 17:11–15; 2 Sam 7:8–16; Ps 132:11–18; Isa 9:7; 11:1–3; Acts 2:29–36; 13:26–36). The Creator and Sustainer of all things, the triune God, remains constant and true. God is the Redeemer who rose victorious over sin and death and reigns as King over all things. The True Story brings meaning to the grand narrative of history and to your life and mine.

Our Worldview Story

Our understanding of the True Story shapes our reading and interpretation of the Bible and the mission of God. It also shapes the way we understand our place and purpose in the world. In other words, the way we understand human life depends on what we believe about God and the human story. We need to ask, "What is the real story of which my life story is a part?" If we believe that the Bible is the true story of the whole world, that God is the Creator and Sustainer of the universe, and that humankind is created in the image of God, then we can begin to answer deeper questions like "Who am I?" "Where am I from?" "Why am I here?" and "What is my purpose?"

N. T. Wright puts it this way: "Worldviews are thus the basic stuff of human existence, the lens through which the world is seen, the blueprint for how one should live in it, and above all the sense of identity and place which enables human beings to be what they are."[4] Our worldview constitutes our basic beliefs, which in turn provide the foundation for the way we engage with the world. Cultivating a missional framework through the lens of the *missio Dei*

---

[4] N. T. Wright, *The New Testament and the People of God* (Minneapolis: Fortress, 1992), 124.

helps us to understand our existence within and our interaction with the world and equips us to engage in meaningful gospel conversations with increasing confidence.

At the beginning of this chapter, I introduced Steiger, the international missionary organization intent on reaching a Global Youth Culture in search of answers to questions like "Who am I?" or "Why am I here?" which correspond to the three core longings discussed in chapter 4. When we consider these questions through the lens of the *missio Dei*, we can share aspects of the good news of God's kingdom directly from the first few chapters of Genesis. If God truly is the Creator of all things, then we are his creation, and we are created in God's image, the *imago Dei.* Since we believe that the Bible is the True Story and provides the blueprint for the *missio Dei*, we can with confidence embrace and participate with people from every tribe, every tongue, every nation in the *missio Dei* and can state with confidence that the gospel is good news for all people.

Reflection

In chapter 1, I demonstrated that Bill Bright interpreted the Great Commission through the lens of revivalists such as William Carey, D. L. Moody, John R. Mott, and Henrietta Mears. Bright's dogged determination to train people in personal evangelism and to help fulfill the Great Commission (Matt 28:18–20) reflects the mid-twentieth-century evangelical context and was anchored in an urgent, premillennial eschatology. He firmly believed that an emphasis on personal evangelism would help to fuel the fulfillment of the Great Commission and save the world from the advancement of communist atheism. *Four Spiritual Laws* offered Christians an easy-to-use tool for presenting both the message of salvation and assurance of salvation.

Bright's strategy was influenced by a framework developed in large part by an earlier, colonial approach to missions, which often relied on parachurch organizations to carry out the task. In addition, it became the missionary's task to spread the gospel from the Christianized West to non-Western and non-Christian areas of the world. Furthermore, *Four Spiritual Laws*, developed in a predominantly Protestant context to communicate assurance of salvation, presumes that a missionary encounter is unnecessary in the Christianized West.

In contrast, if we look at the Great Commission through the lens of the *missio Dei*, we recognize the comprehensive scope of God's authority and Jesus Christ's invitation to participate with the Spirit as witnesses everywhere. This lens, in turn, reveals the fact that the church is missionary by its very nature and is the conduit by which all believers everywhere participate as witnesses in the *missio Dei*. Bearing witness to the good news becomes an integral component of our identity as God's people. The next chapter introduces various narrative approaches to meaningful gospel conversations that have helped me, and I hope they will help you to move from making a presentation to having a conversation.

CHAPTER 6

Cultivating Faithful Recontextualization

L ate in the summer of 2020, I was working feverishly to finish and submit my dissertation. I hoped to graduate in December of 2020. One of my prayers through the PhD process was that I would finish it before my dad passed away. His health had gradually declined during that period. Just a few days before submitting my work to the PhD office, his health took a turn for the worse. Soon I was on a flight to Bozeman where I would join the rest of my family to say goodbye.

On that flight, I reflected on my dad's life and my earnest prayers for his salvation. For forty years, I had prayed that he would surrender his life to Jesus and come to know the deep, deep love of God. He had heard and experienced the gospel through my mom, me, my siblings, his grandchildren, and a host of different friends and acquaintances. He had heard the message of the gospel in a variety of ways, but I was never sure if he had responded to God in faith. On the one hand, I knew that the plan of salvation had been clearly explained to him many times over many years. So, despite not knowing where he stood before God, I held fast to God's faithfulness and promises like those found in 2 Pet 3:8–9:

Dear friends, don't overlook this one fact: with the Lord
one day is like a thousand years, and a thousand years like

one day. The Lord does not delay his promise, as some
understand delay, but is patient with you, not wanting any
to perish, but all to come to repentance.

On the other hand, I also knew that Jesus made it very clear: "No
one can come to me unless the Father who sent me draws him, and I
will raise him up on the last day" (John 6:44).

My dad had been admitted to the hospital for hospice by the
time my sister and I arrived in Bozeman, and throughout the rest of
that day our family took turns going to see him before he was heav-
ily sedated. Throughout the days that followed, since the COVID-19
protocols allowed only one or two family members in his room at
a time, we took turns sitting at his bedside, helping to make him
comfortable as we prayed.

One afternoon, after my shift at his bedside had ended, I sat on
a swing in my brother's backyard. I remember the beautiful Galla-
tin Mountain range that framed the horizon in vivid relief against a
deep blue sky. I wrestled with God. I held two promises in tension—
God wishes that none perish but that all should reach repentance
(2 Pet 3:9), and no one comes to Jesus unless the Father draws him
(John 6:44). Clearly, my dad's life on earth was ending. "Lord, you
have heard our prayers, right? Surely, after all this time, you have
revealed yourself to him. Right?" As I grappled with these truths, I
was overcome by the beguiling and remarkable fact that the measure
of God's love and mercy is boundless. The Spirit of God reassured
me that afternoon, deep down inside, that I could trust God no matter the outcome.

Within a day or so, my dad passed away, and just a day or so
later, we met with his pastor, Dean, to plan a memorial service.
Dean was kind and comforting as he described the friendship that
had developed between him and our dad. He also shared about their

regular lunch meetings where they most often discussed, with the Bible open, dad's desire to love his wife and family well. Who knew?! Later, over the phone, Dean told me that he was confident of my dad's faith in Jesus and shared some of the tangible ways that he had seen him grow in his faith and soften in his demeanor.

Amazingly, God drew my dad to faith in the twilight years of his life through the witness of a faithful pastor. He answered our prayers. I share this story because it demonstrates the redemptive and missionary heart of our triune God and the reality of the *missio Dei*. Never in my wildest of dreams did I think that forty years would pass before my dad would come to faith. In hindsight, I realize that God reveals the truth to us by his grace and in ways we often never dream of. Indeed, "The Lord is not slow to fulfill his promise as some count slowness, but is patient toward you, not wishing that any should perish, but that all should reach repentance" (2 Pet 3:9 ESV). This realization is a fitting place to draw our conversation to a close and to call us to engage in faithful recontextualization in an increasingly secularized context.

Looking Back and Leaning Forward

You might remember that this book began with what I considered to be a compelling question—"Why *Four Spiritual Laws?*" This question emerged from a surprising conversation with a college freshman who had no idea about "what or who" Jesus was. This disruptive conversation, and countless others with all kinds of people, became the seedbed for my master's and PhD studies.

I began the book with a brief introduction of Bill Bright, founder and president of CCC, and the contemporary, historical, theological, and religious influences that shaped what eventually became *Four Spiritual Laws*. To help us understand Bright's context, I provided an overview of his family background, his encounter with revivalist Henrietta Mears, and his faith encounter with God that included a vision and the subsequent founding of CCC. I demonstrated that *Four Spiritual Laws* provided a contextually thoughtful and innovative approach to personal evangelism.

My research also reminded me of Bright's zeal for personal evangelism and his conviction that everyone, everywhere is ready and willing to hear about the love of God. He recognized that Christians lacked training, and *Four Spiritual Laws* provided a simple, straightforward way to share the plan of salvation. My experience as a new believer at the University of Utah—where, in the late 1970s, I learned to share my faith—corroborated Bright's conviction. Over the years, I have presented *Four Spiritual Laws* countless times and have, on occasion, had the opportunity to see people pray to receive Christ—even in my family! However, by the turn of the twenty-first century, my years of experience and well-honed approach had become a barrier to effectively sharing my faith.

Chapter One provided a contrast between Bright's mid-twentieth-century context and ours today. I posed the question, "If it was so easy to believe in God in 1951, why is it so hard for people to believe today?" The chapter includes a snapshot of our current context from four missiological vantage points, highlighting some of the foundational changes that have taken place in our culture and providing helpful categories for our disorientation today.

Vantage Point 1: Introducing Secularization

Vantage Point 2: Cru's Research: "Understanding Faith and Purpose in the City"

Vantage Point 3: Demographic Changes and a Diversity Explosion

Vantage Point 4: Gen Z, the Next Generation.

In chapter 3, I contended that the metanarrative of Scripture, the true story of the whole world, provides a framework for the mission of God—the *missio Dei*. I illustrated ways that the metanarrative of Scripture opens new vistas for gospel conversations in a secularized context. I revisited Cru's research in chapter 4 and revealed a sobering and compelling discovery: While over half of the people surveyed found Christianity either offensive, inauthentic, irrelevant, or unsafe, a surprising 84 percent were willing to have spiritual conversations with Christians. However, most believed that Christians were unwilling and unprepared to participate in discussion with anyone with an opposing point of view. I believe that as followers of Jesus, we must attend carefully to these discoveries and seek to better understand our context and make some serious changes in our behavior.

Cru mined the research and discovered *three core longings* and *five behavior changes* that help us to engage more winsomely with others. I then reimagined my research question, from "How can Cru train others to present the gospel in a twenty-first-century American context and honor Bill Bright's vision and maintain his commitment to evangelism?" to "How can we train Christians to be gospel witnesses in a twenty-first-century American context?"[1]

In chapter 5, I introduced a missional framework and a redemptive way forward. Here, I argued that a robust theological missiology empowers us to be God's witnesses in our twenty-first-century secularized context and provides (1) an interpretive guide or hermeneutic for understanding the storyline of Scripture; (2) a framework that shapes our worldview; and (3) a blueprint for the *missio Dei* that invites us to participate with God as vibrant witnesses. I concluded by demonstrating that a missional framework reframes and enriches

---

[1]   Monaco, "Bill Bright's," xv (see chap. 1, n. 1).

our understanding of the Great Commission. This final chapter deals with the important issue of recontextualizing evangelism.

Recontextualization—Where Do We Go from Here?

My hope is that this book will serve as a marker, a placeholder of sorts, in a conversation that is thousands of years old. God has called and continues to call people just like us to faithfully contextualize our understanding of and approach to communicating the good news.

Bill Bright practiced contextualization by paying critical attention to his particular context, by learning and doing research, and by innovating and experimenting. In fact, we discovered in the first chapter that Bright's *Four Spiritual Laws* emerged from his desire to communicate the love of God and the message of salvation to his predominantly white, Protestant audience. The tools that emerged from his research, including *Four Spiritual Laws*, reflected the use of cutting-edge technology and culturally relevant events and practices. So, it stands to reason that, since America's society and context has changed in dramatic ways, we must confidently engage in faithful recontextualization just like Bill Bright did over seventy years ago.

We have also learned that the Trinity—God the Father, God the Son, and God the Spirit—sustains and promotes the gospel in imaginative and redemptive ways in all kinds of cultures and contexts. The mere fact that we are discussing this topic over 2,000 years after Jesus's resurrection underscores this point. We can rest assured that God's gospel is strong and resilient, which reinforces the fact that the triune God makes contextualization possible. God invites us to be his witnesses in every kind of culture.

Early in the book, I referenced missiologist Paul Hiebert's viewpoint on contextualization, and it bears repeating here. "On the one hand, the gospel belongs to no culture. It is God's revelation of himself and his acts to all people. On the other hand, it must always be understood and expressed within human cultural forms."[2] When we practice contextualization and/or recontextualization, we must beware of the potential to over-contextualize—or over-adapt—our approach to engaging in gospel conversations in the name of cultural relevance. Sometimes we prize innovation and creativity at the expense of our missional hermeneutic.

We must also beware of the danger of undercontextualizing, which often takes place when we resist change in the name of tradition and/or biblical fidelity. Here we run the risk of missing out on new opportunities for gospel engagement. Faithful recontextualization holds these extremes in tensio56.

Four Marks of Faithful Recontextualization

Our missional framework (chapter 5) reinforces the fact that God's Spirit empowers us to be his witnesses, guides our recontextualization, and helps us to guard against over- or under-contextualizing. Faithful recontextualization is a humbling process and requires us to follow the Spirit's lead. The following four marks set the stage for recontextualization. First, we affirm that the church, created by God's Spirit, is meant to reflect the very body of Christ in the world. Second, we respond to God's call by cultivating a confident and prophetic faith. Third, we recognize the need to adopt a *cruciform*

---

[2]   Hiebert, *Anthropological Insights*, 30 (see chap. 1, n. 56).

posture toward evangelism and discipleship. Fourth, we develop a growing awareness of our surroundings.

Mark One: Affirm that the Church Reflects the Body of Christ in the World

The first mark affirms that the church is a visible manifestation of God's kingdom, inaugurated by Jesus at the incarnation. The church is missionary by nature and demonstrates the full power and breadth of God's redemptive work in anticipation of the New Creation.[3]

Significantly, the Spirit of God redeems and transforms individuals and communities through the church. Down through the ages, amid changing cultures and contexts, God's Spirit has always invited the church to participate in the *missio Dei*. Moreover, *every* member of the church is called to participate, not just the paid "professionals." We are *all* God's workmanship, created in Christ Jesus for the good works that God prepared long ago (Eph 2:10).

As we learned in chapter 5, the key to recognizing the Spirit's voice is cultivating a growing understanding of the *missio Dei* and the true story of the whole world. In fact, God's Spirit, sent by the Father and Son, catalyzes the church's witness and provides her with an unprecedented advantage in recontextualization. Jesus, in the upper room discourse, introduces the Spirit who convicts the world about sin, righteousness, and judgment; speaks whatever he hears from the Father; and declares what is to come. God's Spirit, the source of truth, righteousness, and faith, also empowers, guides, and directs the church on mission (John 14:15–17, 25–30; 15:5–7; 16:1–10; Rom 8:1–7, 9–11, 26–30; 1 Cor 2:6–16; 3:16–17; 12:1–11; 2 Cor 3:12–18; 6:14–18; Gal 5:16–25; Eph 1:15–22; 4:17–32; 5:15–21; 2 Pet 1:3–8).

---

[3] Craig Van Gelder, *The Essence of the Church: A Community Created by the Spirit* (Grand Rapids: Baker, 2000), 32.

Newbigin, in his exposition of the Gospel of John, notes, "These promises are part of the preparation of the church for its missionary encounter with all the varied communities and cultures of the world. These are real encounters by which both the world and the church are changed."[4]

Reflection on Mark One

I cannot emphasize enough the importance of reading the Bible to help you to grow in your understanding of the triune God and the *missio Dei*. Rather than purposing to "master the Bible a book at a time," Craig Bartholomew suggests that our desire for God is realized when we listen for God's address—the goal of interpretation.[5] This attentive listening allows us to experience the living and active word of God as that which penetrates our soul and spirit and judges the thoughts and intentions of our heart (Heb 4:12). I recognize, from experience, that reading the Bible can feel daunting one day and boring the next, but it is worth the effort.

Today, we have a variety of ways to engage with God—we can read a physical book, we can listen to books and passages in the Bible on various Bible apps, we can access websites like The Bible Project to help us understand what we are reading. I hope that reading my story and some of the discoveries I have made—well into my sixties—encourages you that it is never too late to listen for God's address through reading or listening to the Bible.

Back in 2019, my friend Susan Goodwin and two of her friends from church decided to host a gathering for the purpose of reading

---

[4]   Lesslie Newbigin, *The Light Has Come: An Exposition of the Fourth Gospel* (Grand Rapids: Eerdmans, 1982), ix.

[5]   Craig G. Bartholomew and David J. H. Beldman, eds., *Hearing the Old Testament: Listening for God's Address* (Grand Rapids: Eerdmans, 2012).

through the Bible. They invited women from their church, their respective neighborhoods, their families, and their spheres of influence to join them one night a week for about thirteen weeks. Their goal was to read through the whole Bible in ninety days. Surprisingly, fifty women showed up at Susan's home, some who had never read one word of the Bible and many who had never read it all the way through. Eventually, due to the encouraging response, Susan and her friends wrote a book, *Every Word: A Reader's 90-Day Guide to the Bible.*[6] It provides a guide for reading through the Bible, checkboxes for tracking progress, and a weekly summary of the week's reading.

Mark Two: Cultivate a Confident and Prophetic Faith

The second mark of faithful recontextualization requires that we cultivate a confident and prophetic faith. Here we learn to rely on God's Spirit who fuels gospel transmission, enables gospel translation in all kinds of cultures and societies, and instigates conversion—the Spirit draws us to God (John 6:44; 1 Cor 2:10; Eph 1:15–19). In addition, cultivating a confident and prophetic faith requires that we shift from making a presentation to having a conversation.

Jesus, just before his ascension and by the Father's authority, promises his disciples that God's Spirit will empower them to be his witnesses from Jerusalem to Judea and Samaria, and to the ends of the earth!

> So, when they had come together, they asked him, "Lord, are you restoring the kingdom to Israel at this time?" He said to them, "It is not for you to know times or periods that the Father has set by his own authority. But you will

---

[6] Susan Goodwin, Jennifer Peterson, and Molly Sawyer, *Every Word: A Reader's 90–Day Guide to the Bible* (Atlanta: CreateSpace, 2019). Available on Amazon and YouVersion.

receive power when the Holy Spirit has come on you, and you will be my witnesses in Jerusalem, in all Judea and Samaria, and to the ends of the earth." (Acts 1:6–8)

Then, at Pentecost, the Spirit unleashed a multilingual and multicultural witness and upended traditional and cultural religious values (Acts 2). This event is followed by Peter's disconcerting vision and his encounter with Cornelius—a Gentile—which underscores the disruption instigated at Pentecost (Acts 10–11). Next, the Jerusalem Council, forced to address the provocative nature of the gospel's spread to the Gentiles, faced an important milestone regarding faithful recontextualization (Acts 15:1–21). Together, they recognized and affirmed that God makes no distinction between Jew and Gentile, but cleanses both by faith (Acts 15:8–9). They determined not to cause difficulties for the Gentiles, "but instead we should write to them to abstain from things polluted by idols, from sexual immorality, from eating anything that has been strangled, and from blood" (Acts 15:20). This summary illustrates how the gospel emerged in different cultures and necessitated recontextualization (Acts 15:10–11, 19–21). God's Spirit empowers us to recontextualize still today.

Another important part of cultivating a confident and prophetic faith requires that we shift from making a presentation to having a conversation. So, amid my research, I asked God to open my eyes, to help me really see the person who pours my coffee, or lives next door, or stands on a street corner holding a sign that says, "Every little bit helps." As I began really looking at the faces and into the eyes of people who serve me at the airport or the dry cleaners, I caught glimpses of the *imago Dei*. These men and women, created in God's image and loved by the Father, are hardwired with a longing for peace, prosperity, and purpose—just like you and me (see chapter 4). Why had I not paid attention before?

Knowing that God calls us to be witnesses, I began to make eye contact with people and ask an ordinary question, "How's your day going?" The most frequent reply? "Nobody ever asks me that question." Often, once people get over the shock, they respond with detailed answers about their complicated lives. I can relate; my life is complicated too. The people we encounter are created and loved by God—just like us. Often, this one simple question leads to a meaningful gospel conversation.

Reflection on Mark Two

In reflection, let me assure you, it has taken me a long time to change my posture—to follow the conversation and not my agenda—and the Five Behavior Changes and Three Core Longings have really helped me to join all kinds of conversations in a whole new way. For example, I have several new friends who long to have children but experience all kinds of anxiety related to finances, timing, or infertility. This longing coupled with anxiety, affects their sense of well-being and calls into question their sense of purpose.

I can relate to these anxieties on a personal level. My husband and I, although we hoped to have children, never did. We endured years of infertility, pursued adoption, and yet remain childless. I cannot begin to tell you how many people God has brought across my path who are experiencing some aspect of infertility. Even as I write this paragraph, I am journeying with a couple of friends who hope to have children. I deeply understand their longing and, even though they do not know God like I do, we often have deep and meaningful gospel conversations. I know what it means to anxiously wait, to grieve month after month, and to consider the prospect of not having children. I also know the power and comfort of God's presence in the hardest seasons of life—even when things do not go our way.

The more transparent and vulnerable I am about my life, the more willing people are to hear about the God I love. Now, many years later, I can talk about the ways Bob and I, as a family of two, experience God's peace and a sense of well-being and purpose. The most profound change I have experienced personally in this process is the freedom to follow the conversation, not my agenda, and to openly bear witness to the faithfulness of God.

Mark Three: A Cruciform Posture

Missiologist Lesslie Newbigin, in the mid-1990s, prophetically maintained that the future of missions "will no longer work along the stream of expanding Western power."[7] We cannot, must not, minimize this significant shift in power. I firmly believe that faithful recontextualization and the future of global missions requires that we adopt a cruciform posture toward evangelism and discipleship—a posture shaped by the cross. It takes courage and humility to go against the grain of our culture and welcome weakness as a position of strength, give way to leaders from other cultures, and embrace suffering and hardship as familiar pathways for the gospel.

STRENGTH IN WEAKNESS

Developing a cruciform approach to evangelism and discipleship is often difficult for those who have characteristically led the charge by raising funds and providing training, tools, and manpower around the world. But remarkably, this cruciform approach permeates the True Story. Paul, as he participates with God's Spirit in the *missio Dei*, exhorts us to imitate Jesus:

---

[7] Lesslie Newbigin, *The Open Secret: An Introduction to the Theology of Mission* (Grand Rapids: Eerdmans, 1995), 5.

Do nothing out of selfish ambition or conceit, but in humility consider others as more important than yourselves. Everyone should look not to his own interests, but rather to the interests of others. Adopt the same attitude as that of Christ Jesus,

who, existing in the form of God,
did not consider equality with God
as something to be exploited.
Instead he emptied himself
by assuming the form of a servant,
taking on the likeness of humanity.
And when he had come as a man,
he humbled himself by becoming obedient
to the point of death—even to death on a cross.
(Phil 2:3–8)

Peter similarly exhorts us to submit to our authorities, to follow in the footsteps of Jesus even in the face of injustice.

For you were called to this, because Christ also suffered for you, leaving you an example, that you should follow in his steps. He did not commit sin, **and no deceit was found in his mouth;** when he was insulted, he did not insult in return; when he suffered, he did not threaten but entrusted himself to the one who judges justly. He himself bore our sins in his body on the tree; so that, having died to sins, we might live for righteousness. **By his wounds you have been healed.** (1 Pet 2:21–24)

God's Spirit is at work from the center to the edges of our lives, and below the surface and often along the margins of society. God often uses suffering and weakness to lay bare our need for the gospel. The apostle Paul, while acknowledging the Spirit as the source of life and freedom (Rom 6:1–14; 8:1–11; 1 Corinthians 2), describes the knowledge of God's glory as a treasure embodied in clay jars "so that this extraordinary power may be from God and not from us" (2 Cor 4:7). This mysterious power is often manifested through us in our affliction, perplexity, persecution, and defeat. "We always carry the death of Jesus in our body, so that the life of Jesus may also be displayed in our body" (2 Cor 4:10). This kind of God-glorifying suffering is central to NT discipleship (Phil 1:15–30; 2:5–11; 3:7–11; Jas 5:7–11; 1 Pet 1:3–11; 2:11–25).

Evangelism and discipleship shaped by the cross provide an outline for meaningful gospel conversations in a secularized age.

MULTICULTURAL AND MULTIETHNIC

Faithful recontextualization necessitates a humble, cruciform way of discipleship that frees us up to learn from our similarities and differences, exercise a cruciform approach to evangelism and discipleship, practice dynamic reconciliation, and pursue unity fused together by God's love (John 13:34–35).

A multicultural and multiethnic hermeneutic is not a political, social, cultural, or institutional issue—it is a gospel issue. The call to oneness in our diversity as followers of Jesus reflects the unity and diversity of the Trinity and is inherent in the *imago Dei*. When Jesus announced the good news of the kingdom of God, he transcended the cultural, political, religious, and social barriers of the day. Some of the most significant moments in the early church happened when the gospel turned long-held cultural traditions and beliefs about food and cleanliness, societal roles, and prejudices upside down. We desperately need each other to correct and expand our understanding of God and the gospel.

SUFFERING AND HARDSHIP

Finally, a cruciform way of discipleship embraces suffering and hardship as pathways for the gospel.

> We also boast in our afflictions, because we know that affliction produces endurance, endurance produces proven character, and proven character produces hope. This hope will not disappoint us, because God's love has been poured out in our hearts through the Spirit who was given to us. (Rom 5:3–5)

Jesus, the Suffering Servant, well acquainted with grief, sets the standard for a cruciform way of evangelism and discipleship.

> Adopt the same attitude as that of Christ Jesus, who, existing in the form of God, did not consider equality with God something to be exploited. Instead he emptied himself by assuming the form of a servant, taking on the likeness of humanity. And when he had come as a man, he humbled himself by becoming obedient to the point of death—even to death on a cross. (Phil 2:5–8)

The COVID-19 pandemic heightened our awareness of disappointment, hardship, suffering, and death all over the world. In the United States, polarizing politics, racism, and social disparities came into full view and caused some people to question God, their faith, and even the meaning of the gospel. We must continue to engage in these kinds of conversations, because the gospel is resilient. And because people the world over experience doubt and grief and struggle with pain and suffering just like we do—by faith.

Reflection on Mark Three

My journey over the past decade has been shaped by a growing understanding of the multicultural and multiethnic demographics in America from a statistical point of view, but more importantly, from a human one. In chapter 1, I introduced the Evangelism Think Tank that formed early in my PhD research. Our ethnically diverse group of about ten people included Cru staff from the Campus Ministry, Athletes in Action, and City and ranged in age from twenty-eight to sixty. Together we pressed into many of the topics I address in this book, and our different life experiences and points of view challenged and helped to shape our understanding of Bright's context as compared to today's. The fact that Bright's context included the end of WWII, the end of Japanese internment in the US, and the beginnings of the civil rights movement took on new meaning because of the group's different backgrounds and experiences.

Before the formation of the Think Tank and during my master's research, I experienced a particularly poignant and humbling moment when I visited Cru Inner City's office in Chicago in 2012. Milton Massie, the director, took me on a tour of Chicago's South Side. He explained to me the effects of gun violence in their neighborhood and pointed out the negative effects of gentrification. He also shared the history of Cru Inner City and explained their commitment to serving the local church and pastors in their community.

Etched in my memory is the conversation we had toward the end of my visit. Milton remarked, "Cas, you and I are unlikely friends." He was right. I had never been exposed to an urban setting like his, and before that day, I had no idea what gentrification was.

I was raised in a white, upper-middle-class home, and, to my best recollection, Milton was among the first Black friends I had ever had. I am learning that a cruciform approach to faithful recontextualization requires humility and a willingness to see things from someone else's perspective, and also kindness and grace like I experienced from Milton. My life is richer because of that experience and because of his witness in showing me a whole different side to the gospel.

Understanding another person's story, no matter our ethnic or cultural background, takes time and a willingness to consciously engage with people different from us. For me, as a middle-aged white woman, my exposure to the Japanese Internment Museum in Portland, OR, the Human and Civil Rights Museum in Atlanta, GA, and the Trail of Tears severely impacting Native Americans in the early-to-mid-ninteenth century informed my limited perspective on racism in profound ways. These discoveries have also opened the door for ongoing meaningful gospel conversations.

My friend Cynthia often reminded me, "You do not know what you do not know." Her words ring true—there is so much we do not know about each other.

For faithful recontextualization to take place, we must remember that by God's design we, the body of Christ, are meant to reflect the multi-ethnic and multi-cultural world God created. Stepping into each other's shoes and seeking to understand one another's story epitomizes a cruciform posture.

Mark Four: Develop a Growing Awareness of Our Surroundings
Remember, in chapter 4 we celebrated the fact that while most people are willing to talk to Christians about spiritual things, most believed that Christians only reluctantly converse with people holding a different point of view. The fourth mark of faithful recontextualization

urges us to develop a growing awareness of our culture. This growing awareness enables us to more easily engage with people who hold different points of view—the gospel is good news for all people and helps us to avoid either under- or overcontextualization.

This is powerfully demonstrated by Peter's vision in Acts 10 (introduced earlier in this chapter) where he is told by God to "kill and eat" food that was impure and ritually unclean (Acts 10:14). We see by Peter's response that this request made absolutely no sense—God repeated it three times before Peter relented. Then, to make matters even more perplexing for Peter, God summons him to go to the house of Cornelius—a Gentile (Acts 10:9–16, 28–29). Once Peter arrives at the home of Cornelius, he realizes the significance of this event. No less remarkable is God's invitation to Cornelius, who, while praying to God, received instructions to send for Peter, a Jew.

This example demonstrates God's impartiality: "The Holy Spirit came down on all those who heard the message" (Acts 10:44). Peter and Cornelius's encounter illustrates cultural awareness, agility, and faith. Their respective decisions transformed them both.

Reflection

I purposely use the phrase True Story of the Whole World (True Story) to reinforce the fact that the metanarrative of Scripture is neither a myth nor a fable, nor simply a better story that competes with other religious stories, but is, in fact, true. We must remember that the True Story permeates all of life and gives us confidence in the public square.

Inherent in my claim is the assumption that there are other stories at work out there in our society that look and even feel true, and they challenge the fidelity of the True Story. In chapter 3 we looked at Ariana Grande's pop single and perfume, "God is a Woman." I pointed out how this bold assertion reflects a secularized point of view rife with the prominent ideology of expressive individualism. In other words, the title and lyrics reveal something of Grande's truest self—something that we cannot deny. I included in the same chapter Gabby Bernstein's declaration, "The Universe Has Your Back." Her spirituality is a mix of pantheism, self-help, New Age, and expressive individualism. She encourages her followers to discover their destiny by finding themselves.

In chapter 5 I introduced Steiger International, a missionary organization that seeks to reach the Global Youth Culture. Steiger has identified at least five lies that the Global Youth Culture believes, each of which lends insight into our cultural and societal surroundings. The first lie is embedded in our secularized culture: "We can only be sure of what we see." This fable is predicated on the notion that truth is relative to each person, but it leaves our deepest questions forever unanswered—"Who am I?" "Why am I here?" and "What is my purpose?" Second, since there are no answers for our deepest questions, then logically speaking, "We must be here by accident." In other words, since there's no grand purpose for this life, it doesn't really matter who I am or what I do. The third lie, "We can be whoever we want to be," might promise a sense of personal freedom, but in truth, this statement seldom proves to be true.

Fourth, there is the lie, "Everything is going to be okay." This ignores the staggering rise in mental health issues, drug addiction, and suicide. It makes light of the challenges everyone faces in this life. To believe this lie leads to an endless search for something, anything, to assuage our fears and anxiety. A fifth lie, "Love is just a passing feeling," suggests that relationships are fluid; they change all the time and leave no possibility of true companionship. In my research and experience, I have discovered that these lies affect not only the Global Youth Culture but persons of almost every age, including you and me.

Cultivating cultural awareness provides us with opportunities to learn about God and ourselves, to utilize our missional framework in meaningful ways, and to enter conversations in relevant ways. In fact, I have discovered the importance of drawing from the doctrine of creation. When I interact with people who are grappling with serious questions related to their origin and identity, I often turn to Genesis 1–3 and share the creation story. When I have conversations about infertility or personal worth, I love to read from Psalm 139 and introduce my friends to the God who created them and is intimately acquainted with all their ways.

How Do We Respond?

Discover or Rediscover the True Story of the Whole World
I underscore the need to read the Bible not simply because it is a good book to read, but because within its pages we discover the triune God and Jesus Christ, the clue to human history and the source of meaning for our lives. We have been created for a purpose whether we are plumbers or potters, students or solar engineers, parents, pastors, or caregivers. Here are a few books that have helped me to better understand the True Story.

1. *The Jesus Storybook Bible: Every Story Whispers His Name*, by Sally Lloyd Jones, is a children's Bible with the profound message of God's love at its heart and is a great place to start.

2. *The 30-Minute Bible: God's Story for Everyone*, by Craig Bartholomew and Paige Vanosky, explains the True

Story by highlighting the four themes and six acts I mentioned in chapter 3.

3. *The True Story of the Whole World: Finding Your Place in God's Story*, by Michael Goheen and Craig Bartholomew, provides a more in-depth look at the True Story than the *30-Minute Bible* and explains in more detail the six acts.

If you learn better by watching a video, these are excellent and engaging resources that are free and accessible no matter your learning style:

1. *The Gospel Project* (https://www.gospelproject.com) provides Christ-centered, chronological Bible studies for kids, adults, and students.

2. *The Bible Project* (https://www.bibleproject.com) is an excellent resource, especially if you are a visual learner, that provides short videos that explain the metanarrative of Scripture, the Trinity, the incarnation, the role of the Spirit, and so much more.

Three Core Longings, Five Behavior Changes, Three-Statement Stories

As you continue to get to know the triune God of the Bible and better understand the True Story, take some time to review the three core longings introduced in chapter 4. Identify your core longings and start to articulate the ways God helps you when you feel anxious, or when you are unsure where your next meal is coming from, or when you lack a sense of security for your family, or when you lose or find your sense of purpose. Honestly, growing in our awareness of our longings helps us to interact with God on a deeper level and cultivates humility—we are needy, fearful, and anxious, too, and need love and reassurance.

Next, review the five behavior changes also discussed in chapter 4. Write them on a Post-It or set a reminder on your phone to prompt you to change your conversational behavior. The art of listening well and conversing with people who hold differing opinions is not always easy, but the five behavior changes are a great place to start. I want to emphasize here that our cultural context requires compassion and understanding, and we must maintain the posture of genuine learners.

Gather some friends together and work on three-statement testimonies—or "today" testimonies—because it helps to make a conscious effort to acknowledge or remember specific ways God has intervened in our lives. But it is one thing to take note of those instances, and it is a whole new step to talk about it—so start with your friends.

Make New Friends

I had the opportunity to introduce MyFriends Lifestyle, an innovative approach to gospel conversations, at a training session in February 2020. MyFriends Lifestyle is an invitation to a "gospel way of life." It is not a strategy. The online training helps us learn how to invite friends who might not ever attend church to discover Jesus with us. MyFriends Lifestyle provides simple ideas for starting conversations in our networks of influence in a faith-filled way.

We launched a learning community of twenty Cru staff to try out MyFriends Lifestyle in our contexts in cities all around the country. Then, fourteen days later, the COVID-19 pandemic overturned our plans. The pandemic forced us to put our training into action in a more holistic way. Some of us delivered food to our homebound neighbors, others hosted socially distanced gatherings in backyards, and several cared for neighbors and friends who were sick, hospitalized, or experiencing mental health challenges.

One guy in our learning community started an online "Discovery Group" with his neighbors and had the opportunity to cultivate new friendships with neighbors he had never met before the pandemic. They talked about mental health, marriage, and Jesus. He continues, still today, to reap the rewards of those opportunities! The MyFriends approach prompted my husband and me to get to know some of our neighbors. During the pandemic we started a weekly prayer time at our neighborhood gazebo and prayed for people facing business closures, family breakdowns, and health crises. We made friends with a couple who had recently moved to the United States from India who described feeling "profoundly lonely." MyFriends provided a fresh approach for our learning community to cultivate a gospel way of life in the face of hardship, isolation, and suffering.

To the seasoned evangelist, MyFriends Lifestyle may seem anticlimactic. However, we experienced multifaceted benefits. First, it reminds us to make friends with our neighbors. It also encourages us to talk freely and openly about the God we love, to share about our highs *and* lows. MyFriends also reminds us to pay attention to the Spirit's promptings—sometimes he calls us to respond in unconventional and maybe even irrational ways. I find that the Spirit often prompts me to call or text someone out of the blue, and often (but not always) there is a tangible reason behind the prompt. One participant described a prompt to buy groceries for someone who, it turned out, was in great need. Other times the Spirit might urge us to show up in unplanned and unchoreographed ways. MyFriends allows us and others to experience God firsthand and reminds us, in simple ways, of the unprecedented opportunity to live into our faith and walk with God alongside people who are at different points along the journey to knowing God.

Perhaps most profoundly for me, I learned, all over again, how to make friends. For most of my adult life, I have been surrounded with friends who share my beliefs. MyFriends opened my eyes to the privilege of making new friends, of living out my faith in every relationship and encounter. I hope this encourages you to do the same.

Conclusion

I began this book with a question that propelled me into missiology: "Why *Four Spiritual Laws*?" I have devoted most of my time and energy to answering that question. I introduced Bill Bright, the developer of *Four Spiritual Laws*, and demonstrated the various influences and factors that shaped him and this approach to evangelism. I knew Bill Bright, I respected him as a leader, and I contend that we should follow in his footsteps and contextualize our approach to evangelism with the same zeal and conviction he modeled for us.

I have demonstrated that our secularized twenty-first-century context is vastly different from Bright's, and I further contend that, to follow in his footsteps, we must develop a narrative approach to gospel conversations. I firmly believe that the complexity of today's context and the questions that are being raised require a robust missiological theology that provides us with a deeper understanding of the triune God and the true story of the whole world. I continue to devote myself to the development of a missional framework and invite you to join this conversation and include me in the conversations you are having wherever you are.

Recommended Reading

The following publications provide a small sampling of the topics covered in this manuscript in addition to the sources cited and are recommended for further reading if you are interested. For a more comprehensive bibliography, contact me at cas.monaco.com.

Missiology and Theology

Bartholomew, Craig G., and Michael W. Goheen. *The Drama of Scripture: Finding Our Place in the Biblical Story.* Grand Rapids: Baker Academic, 2014.

> *The Drama of Scripture* presents the true story of the whole world as a comprehensive narrative of God's redemptive work across the canon. This publication provides a more in-depth look at the *True Story of the Whole World: Finding Your Place in the Biblical Drama* by the same authors.

Gonzales, Justo. *Mañana: Christian Theology from a Hispanic Perspective.* Nashville: Abington, 1990.

> Gonzales, a historical theologian, provides a analysis of the development of Christian theology and tradition through Hispanic eyes. Gonzales has been a conversation partner of sorts for me along the way and I have benefited from his perspective and scholarship.

Hirsch, Alan, and Rob Kelly. *Metanoia: How God Radically Transforms People, Churches, and Organizations from the Inside
Out.* 100 Movements Publishing, 2023.

Hirsch and Kelly provide a provocative, theologically rich,
and thoughtful analysis of our current reality and invite us to
embark on a "Metanoia Journey"—a journey of repentance.
Their approach, as refreshing as it is startling, urges both a
healthy pause and deep, Spirit-led examination. This pairs well
with chapter 2's reality check and provides another facet to
chapter 6's recontextualization.

Van Gelder, Craig, and Dwight J. Zscheile. *Participating in God's
Mission: A Theological Missiology for the Church in America.*
Grand Rapids: Eerdmans, 2018.

Van Gelder and Zscheile demonstrate how missiology provides a framework for church participation in an era of unrav-
eling and change. This scholarly publication provides insight
into chapter 1's focus on Bright's twenty-first-century context,
chapter 5's Missional Framework, and chapter 6's call for
recontextualization.

Williams, Jarvis J. *Redemptive Kingdom Diversity: A Biblical Theology of the People of God.* Grand Rapids: Baker, 2021.

Williams's work offers a timely and comprehensive survey
of the diverse people of God from Genesis to Revelation and
applies his overview in a timely way to race, racism, and
ethnicity. This publication adds theological perspective to the
metanarrative of Scripture.

Wright, Christopher J. H. *The Mission of God: Unlocking the Bible's Grand Narrative*. Downers Grove: IVP Academic, 2006.

Wright's masterful work presents the Biblical narrative through the lens of the mission of God across the metanarrative of Scripture and demonstrates that the Church is designed to participate with God in mission. *The Mission of God* is a hefty read and provides rich insight into the mission of God, particularly in the OT.

Secularization

Smith, James K. A. *How (Not) to Be Secular: Reading Charles Taylor*. Grand Rapids: Eerdmans, 2014.

Smith takes an engaging and accessible look at Charles Taylor's *A Secular Age* and provides a reading guide to philosophy and Taylor's more complex words, phrases, and arguments.

Taylor, Charles. *A Secular Age*. Cambridge: Belknap, 2007.

Taylor describes our era as one in which people find belief in God not only implausible but unimaginable and view the world based entirely on what they can explain or experience without any reference to God. Taylor's secularism is not void of spirituality but treats Christianity as just one option among an explosion of others. Taylor, in this daunting publication, takes the reader on a journey across history and demonstrates how the secularization described above emerged.

Evangelism, Apologetics, and Worldview

Guinness, Os. *Fool's Talk: Recovering the Art of Christian Persuasion.* Downers Grove: IVP, 2015.

Guinness provides an insightful look at the art and science of creative persuasion. He argues that Christians are weak in the art of persuasion and struggle to converse with people who have different points of view.

Newbigin, Lesslie. *Foolishness to the Greeks: The Gospel and Western Culture.* Grand Rapids: Eerdmans, 1986.

Newbigin's work explores the gospel and Western culture and poses this haunting question: "What would be involved in a genuinely missionary encounter between the gospel and this whole way of perceiving, thinking, and living that we call 'modern Western culture'? This short book is deeply thought-provoking and well worth the read.

Goheen, Michael W., and Craig G. Bartholomew. *Living at the Crossroads: An Introduction to Christian Worldview.* Grand Rapids: Baker Academic, 2008.

Goheen and Bartholomew trace the origin of the word *worldview* and take a close look at the origins of Western culture and Western thought. They explore the dynamic relationship between gospel and culture by introducing a biblical and cultural worldview, and a worldview in action. The reader is encouraged to pay attention to the beliefs that shape culture today and encourage gospel engagement.

Cultivating Cultural Awareness

Costanzo, Eric, Daniel Yang, Matthew Soerens. *Inalienable: How Marginalized Kingdom Voices Can Help Save the American Church.* Downers Grove: IVP, 2022.

Together, Costanzo, Yang, and Soerens, from different but harmonious perspectives, challenge us to restore health to the church in America by "decentering" ourselves from American idols and "recentering" on God and God's kingdom. With the ancient church, global Christians and the poor as our guides, they call us to find hope from the margins and reimagine gospel witness.

Newbell, Trillia J. *United: Captured by God's Vision for Diversity.* Chicago: Moody, 2016.

Newbell invites her readers to join her in pursuing the joys of diversity through her own stories and that reflect her theology of diversity in very real and practical ways.

Pei, Adrian. *The Minority Experience: Navigating Emotional and Organizational Realities.* Downers Grove: IVP, 2018.

Pei is an organizational consultant whose work focuses on the key challenges ethnic minorities face in majority-culture organizations. I had the privilege of working with Adrian in Cru for a while and our discussion around his work added to my learning and understanding as an organizational leader.

Bibliography

Ashford, Bruce Riley, and Heath A. Thomas. *The Gospel of Our King: Bible, Worldview, and the Mission of Every Christian.* Grand Rapids: Baker Academic, 2019.

Bailey, Sarah. "Campus Crusade Changes Name to Cru." *Christianity Today*, July 19, 2011. http://www.christianitytoday.com/ct/2011/julyweb-only/campus-crusade-name-change.html.

Baker, William H. "Secularist, Secularism." Page 865 in *Evangelical Dictionary of World Missions*. Edited by A. Scott Moreau. Grand Rapids: Baker, 2000.

Barna Group. *Gen Z: The Culture, Beliefs and Motivations Shaping the Next Generation.* Ventura, CA: Barna Group, 2018.

Bartholomew, Craig G., and Michael W. Goheen. *The Drama of Scripture: Finding Our Place in the Biblical Story.* Grand Rapids: Baker Academic, 2014.

———. *The True Story of the Whole World: Finding Your Place in the Biblical Drama.* Grand Rapids: Faith Alive Christian Resources, 2004.

Bartholomew, Craig G., and Paige P. Vanosky. *The 30-Minute Bible: God's Story for Everyone.* Downers Grove: IVP, 2021.

Beougher, Timothy K. "Moody, Dwight Lyman." Page 657 in *Evangelical Dictionary of World Missions*, Edited by A. Scott Moreau. Grand Rapids: Baker, 2000.

Bergquist, Linda, and Michael D. Crane. *City Shaped Churches: Planting Churches in the Global Era.* Skyforest, CA: Urban Loft, 2018.

Bernstein, Gabby. "Meet Gabby." https://gabbybernstein.com/meet-gabby.

———. "How to Trust the Universe." https://gabbyberstein.com/
how-to-trust-the-universe/.

———. *The Universe Has Your Back: Transform Fear to Faith.*
Carlsbad, CA: Hay House Publishing, 2016.

Bright, Bill. *A Handbook for Christian Maturity: Ten Basic Steps
Toward Christian Maturity.* Orlando: New Life Publications,
1994.

———. "A Strategy for Fulfilling the Great Commission." Dallas
Lay Institute of Evangelism, February 13–20, 1966, Campus
Crusade for Christ Archives, Orlando, FL.

———. *Come Help Change the World.* Peachtree, GA: Bright
Media Foundation and Campus Crusade for Christ, 1999.
Kindle edition.

———. *Four Spiritual Laws.* Los Angeles: Campus Crusade for
Christ, 1964.

———. "Methods and Philosophy of Personal Evangelism," pre-
sented at the World Congress on Evangelism, Kongresshalle,
Berlin, October 26–November 4, 1966, Campus Crusade for
Christ Archives, Orlando, FL.

———. "Student Power, The Campus Ministry of Campus Crusade for Christ." *Action Magazine: A Special Report* 1, no. 1
(Spring 1969): 8.

Budiman, Abby. "Key Findings About U.S. Immigrants."
The Pew Research Center, August 20, 2020. https://
www.pewresearch.org/short-reads/2020/08/20/
key-findings-about-u-s-immigrants/.

Carpenter, Joel. *Revive Us Again: The Reawakening of American
Fundamentalism.* New York: Oxford University Press, 1997.

Cru. "I Am From." https://sites.cru.org/culturalconversationcards/
elementor-173/.

————. "Perspective Cards." https://www.cru.org/us/en/train-and-grow/share-the-gospel/outreach-strategies/perspectivecards.html.

————. "Soularium." https://www.cru.org/us/en/train-and-grow/share-the-gospel/outreach-strategies/soularium/soularium-overview.html.

Elmore, Tim, and Andrew McPeak. *Generation Z: Unfiltered.* Atlanta: Poet Gardner, 2019. Kindle edition.

Frey, William H. *Diversity Explosion: How New Racial Demographics are Remaking America.* Washington, DC: Brookings Institution Press, 2018.

Gallup. "Religion: Survey of American's population from 1948–2014." https://news.gallup.com/poll/1690/religion.aspx.

Goheen, Michael W., and Craig G. Bartholomew. *Living at the Crossroads: An Introduction to Christian Worldview.* Grand Rapids: Baker Academic, 2008.

Goodwin, Susan, Jennifer Peterson, and Molly Sawyer. *Every Word: A Reader's 90–day Guide to the Bible.* Atlanta: CreateSpace, 2019.

————. *Every Word: A Reader's 90–day Guide to the Bible*, YouVersion. Portland, OR: The Bible Project, 2019.

Guinness, Os. *Fool's Talk: Recovering the Art of Christian Persuasion.* Downers Grove: IVP, 2015.

Hiebert, Paul G. *Anthropological Insights for Missionaries.* Grand Rapids: Baker Academic, 1986.

Hirsch, Alan, and Rob Kelly. *Metanoia: How God Radically Transforms People, Churches, and Organizations from the Inside Out.* 100 Movements Publishing, 2023.

Hunter, James Davison. Introduction to *My Life among the Deathworks: Illustrations of the Aesthetics of Authority*, by Philip

Rieff, xv–xxviii. Charlottesville: University of Virginia Press, 2006.

Kahn, Richard, and Douglas Kellner. "Global Youth Culture." UCLA, August 29, 2006. https://pages.gseis.ucla.edu/faculty/kellner/essays/globyouthcult.pdf.

Lloyd Jones, Sally. *The Jesus Storybook Bible: Every Story Whispers His Name.* Grand Rapids: Zondervan, 2007.

Loritts, Brian. *Insider Outsider: My Journey as a Stranger in White Evangelicalism and My Hope for Us All.* Grand Rapids: Zondervan, 2018.

Madden, Andrea V. B. "Henrietta C. Mears 1890–1963." Master's thesis, Gordon-Conwell Theological Seminary, 1997.

McDowell, Josh. *More Than A Carpenter.* San Francisco: Living Books, 1986.

———. "My Story: Josh McDowell." Cru, My Story: How My Life Changed. https://www.cru.org/us/en/how-to-know-god/my-story-a-life-changed/my-story-josh-mcdowell.html.

———. *The Resurrection Factor.* Crownhill, Milton Keynes, UK: Authentic Media, 2005.

McDowell, Josh, and Sean McDowell. *Evidence That Demands A Verdict.* Nashville: Thomas Nelson, 2017.

Monaco, Cas. "Bill Bright's (1921–2003) *Four Spiritual Laws* Reimagined: A Narrative Approach to Meaningful Gospel Conversations for an American Twenty-First-Century Secularized Context." PhD diss. Southeastern Baptist Theological Seminary, 2020.

Monaco, Cas, Melanie Krumrey, Yamit Saliceti, and Pam Strain. "1 Peter Miniseries: Finding the True Story in Your Story." https://casmonaco.com/1-peter.

Monaco, Cas and Gary Runn. "Scattering Seeds: Moments and Conversations." The Send Institute, July 16, 2018. https://www.sendinstitute.org/scattering-gospel-seeds/.

"The Most Important Question Ever Asked: Answer Unknown by 89.1%." Page 11 in *The Collegiate Challenge Magazine,* no. 1, (May 1964). Campus Crusade for Christ Archives, Orlando, FL

"MyFriends Lifestyle." https://myfriends.life/.

Newbell, Trillia J. *United: Captured by God's Vision for Diversity.* Chicago: Moody, 2016.

Newbigin, Lesslie. *Foolishness to the Greeks: The Gospel and Western Culture.* Grand Rapids: Eerdmans, 1986.

———. *The Light Has Come: An Exposition of the Fourth Gospel.* Grand Rapids: Eerdmans, 1982.

———. *The Open Secret: An Introduction to the Theology of Mission.* Grand Rapids: Eerdmans, 1995.

Pei, Adrian. *The Minority Experience: Navigating Emotional and Organizational Realities.* Downers Grove: InterVaristy, 2018.

Powers, Barbara Hudson. *The Henrietta Mears Story.* Westwood, NJ: Fleming H. Revell, 1957.

Richardson, Michael Lewis. *Amazing Faith: The Authorized Biography of Bill Bright.* Colorado Springs: WaterBrook, 2000.

Rieff, Philip. *My Life among the Deathworks: Illustrations of the Aesthetics of Authority.* Vol. 1 of *Sacred Order/Social Order.* Edited by Kenneth S. Piver. Charlottesville: University of Virginia Press, 2006.

Sire, James. *Naming the Elephant: Worldview As a Concept.* Downers Grove: IVP Academic, 2004.

———. *The Universe Next Door: A Basic Worldview Catalog.* Downers Grove: IVP, 1997.

Smith, James K. A. *How (Not) to Be Secular: Reading Charles Taylor.* Grand Rapids: Eerdmans, 2014.

Smith, Wilbur. Letter of Endorsement, June 22, 1951, Campus Crusade for Christ Archives, Orlando, FL.

Taylor, Charles. *A Secular Age*. Cambridge: Belknap, 2007.

"The Bible Project." https://www.bibleproject.com.

"The Gospel Project." https://www.gospelproject.com.

Turner, John G. *Bill Bright and Campus Crusade for Christ: The Renewal of Evangelicalism in Postwar America*. Chapel Hill: University of North Carolina Press, 2008. Kindle edition.

Van Gelder, Craig. *The Essence of the Church: A Community Created by the Spirit*. Grand Rapids: Baker, 2000.

Van Gelder, Craig, and Dwight J. Zscheile. *Participating in God's Mission: A Theological Missiology for the Church in America*. Grand Rapids: Eerdmans, 2018.

White, James Emery. *Meet Gen Z: Understanding and Reaching the New Post-Christian World*. Grand Rapids: Baker, 2017.

Williams, Jarvis J. *Redemptive Kingdom Diversity: A Biblical Theology of the People of God*. Grand Rapids: Baker, 2021.

Wright, Brooke, Rick Fossum, Neil Bedwell, and Gail Brooks. "Understanding Faith and Purpose in the City." Atlanta: Cyrano Marketing Collective, 2016.

Wright, Christopher J. H. *The Mission of God: Unlocking the Bible's Grand Narrative*. Downers Grove: IVP Academic, 2006.

Wright, N. T. *Scripture and the Authority of God: How to Read the Bible Today*. New York: HarperCollins, 2013.

———. *The New Testament and the People of God*. Philadelphia: Fortress, 1992.

Name and Subject Index

A

Abraham   *44, 51–52, 83, 85, 88–89*

Adam and Eve   *49–50, 66, 88*

Ashford, Bruce
  Gospel of Our King   48

atheism   *14, 17, 36, 91*

B

Barna Group   *34–37, 125*

Bartholomew, Craig G.
  Drama of Scripture, The: Finding Our Place in the Biblical Story   119
  Hearing the Old Testament: Listening for God's Address   101
  Living at the Crossroads: An Introduction to Christian Worldview   122
  Thirty-Minute Bible, The: God's Story for Everyone   66, 113
  True Story of the Whole World, The   44, 16, 114

Beldman, David J. H.   *101*

Bergquist, Linda

City Shaped Churches: Planting Churches in the Global Era   34

Bernstein, Gabrielle   *58, 112*

Bible   *43–46, 49, 54, 60–61, 62–64, 67, 80–81, 88, 90–91, 101–2, 113–14*

Bible Project, The   114–15

Bosch, David J.
  Transforming Mission: Paradigm Shifts in Theology of Mission   7–8

Bright, Bill   *1–6, 8–10, 12–21, 14, 17–18, 20–21, 25, 28, 35, 56, 62–63, 80, 91, 95, 97, 109, 117–18, 120*
  Four Spiritual Laws   1–4, 10, 12–18, 16–21, 25, 27–28, 63, 91–92, 95–96, 98, 117

Bright, Forrest Dale   *4*

Bright, Samuel   *4*

Bright, Vonette   *28*

Budiman, Abby
  "Key Findings about U.S. Immigrants"   *33*

C

Campus Crusade for Christ (Cru)   *1–3, 12–13, 21,*

28–29, 41, 60, 62, 64, 72, 95, 109, 115

Evangelism Think Tank   3, 109

Family Life   77

Soularium   77–78

Carey, William   6–7, 91

Christianity   7, 26, 29–30, 56, 63–65, 71, 73, 97, 121

Christians   6, 15–16, 25, 34, 62, 65, 69, 73, 79, 91, 96–97, 110

church, the   7, 34, 38, 53–54, 61–62, 82, 84, 92, 99–102, 107, 109, 115

civil rights movement   8, 109

communism   8, 14, 17, 21

contextualization   3, 20–21, 28, 35, 87, 98, 117

over-contextualizing   99

recontextualizing   1, 3–19, 95, 98, 99–100, 102–3, 105, 107, 110

undercontextualizing   21, 99

Costanzo, Eric

Inalienable: How Marginalized Kingdom Voices Can Help Save the American Church   123

COVID-19   68, 70–71, 78, 94, 108, 115

Crane, Michael

City Shaped Churches: Planting Churches in the Global Era   34

Creation   43, 44, 46–50, 55–56, 65, 81–82, 84–87, 91, 113

New   44–46, 53–56, 65, 84, 100

Creator   48–51, 68, 84–86, 90–91

D

David (King)   45, 47, 52, 90

discipleship   11–12, 100, 105, 107–8

E

Elmore, Tim

Generation Z: Unfiltered   36

evangelism   1–3, 5–21, 25, 28–29, 34, 62–63, 91, 96–98, 100, 105, 107–9, 117, 122

Evans, Louis Jr.   9

F

faith   1, 10, 18–20, 23, 29, 38, 41–42, 52, 56, 65, 70–71, 73–74, 93, 95–96, 99–100, 102–3, 108–10, 117

families   37, 47, 56, 69

Father, God the   42, 48, 53, 69, 81–82, 94, 98, 100, 102

First Presbyterian Church of Hollywood   5, 10, 12

five behavior changes   69–71, 104, 114

five lies   112–13

Frey, William

Diversity Explosion: How New Racial Demographics are Remaking America   33
Fuller, Charles E.   5

G

Gen Z   *24, 34–38*
Global Youth Culture   *78, 91, 112–13*
Goheen, Michael W.
  Drama of Scripture, The: Finding Our Place in the Biblical Story   119
  Living at the Crossroads: An Introduction to Christian Worldview   122
  True Story of the Whole World, The   114
Goodwin, Susan
  Every Word: A 90-day Guide to the Bible   101
gospel, the   *1–3, 6, 10, 15–16, 20–21, 39, 43–44, 51, 60, 62, 64, 71–72, 74–75, 79–80, 82, 91–93, 97–99, 102–3, 105, 107–8, 110, 122*
Gospel Project, the   *114–115*
Grande, Ariana   *57, 59, 111*
Great Commission   *3, 6–7, 10–15, 21, 28, 80, 91–92, 98*
Guinness, Ôs
  Fool's Talk: Recovering the Art of Christian Persuasion   122

H

Halverson, Richard   *9*
Hiebert, Paul   *99*
  Anthropological Insights for Missionaries   20
Hinduism   *62*
Hirsch, Alan
  Metanoia: How God Radically Transforms People, Churches, and Organizations from the Inside Out   120
Holy Spirit   *11, 16, 43, 45, 48, 53, 69, 74, 81–83, 86, 92, 94, 98–100, 102–3, 105, 107–8, 111, 114, 116*
humanism   *25, 27, 59, 63*

I

imago Dei (God's image)   *43, 47–49, 48, 67, 79, 103, 107*
Isaiah (prophet)   *45, 50, 52, 83, 86*
Israel   *44, 46–48, 52, 85, 89–90, 102*

J

Jesus Christ   *2, 5–6, 10, 15–19, 29, 31–32, 35, 42, 45–46, 48–49, 52–55, 61–65, 69–74, 72, 74, 79, 81–84, 86–87, 92–95, 97–98, 100, 102, 105–8, 113, 115*
  crucifixion   *82–83*
  incarnation   *45, 52, 82, 100, 114*

King   *48, 52, 83, 87, 90*
Lord   *6, 13, 18, 45, 57, 85,
        87–88, 93–95, 102*
resurrection   *19, 82–83, 98*
Savior   *6, 18*
Son of David   *90*
Son of Man   *52, 82–83, 86*
Suffering Servant   *45, 52–53,
        83, 108*
Jones, Sally Lloyd
    Jesus Storybook Bible, The   *45,
        113*

K

Kelly, Rob
    *Metanoia: How God
        Radically Transforms
        People, Churches, and
        Organizations from the
        Inside Out*   *120*
Kingdom, God's   *46, 48–49, 53,
        82, 86, 91, 100, 107*

M

Massie, Milton   *109–10*
McDowell, Josh   *19*
    *Evidence that Demands A
        Verdict*   *19*
    More Than a Carpenter   *19*
    Resurrection Factor, The   *19*
Mears, Henrietta   *3–5, 9–12, 28,
        63, 91, 96*

missio Dei (mission of God)   *43–
        44, 51, 53, 79–82, 88, 90–91,
        95, 97, 100–1, 105*
Monaco, Cas
    "Bill Bright's (1921–2003)
        Four Spiritual Laws
        Reimagined: A Narrative
        Approach to Meaningful
        Gospel Conversations
        for an American Twenty-
        First-Century Secularized
        Context."   *2, 25, 28, 30,
        62*
    "Scattering Gospel Seeds:
        Moments and
        Conversations'   *72*
Moody, D. L.   *7–8, 91*
Moses   *44, 47, 52, 89*
Mott, John R.   *91*
    *Evangelization of the World in
        This Generation, The*   *8*
MyFriends Lifestyle   *115–16*

N

Newbell, Trillia J
    *United: Captured by God's
        Vision for Diversity*   *123*
Newbigin, Lesslie
    *Foolishness to the Greeks:
        The Gospel and Western
        Culture*   *122*

Light Has Come, The: An Exposition of the Fourth Gospel   101

Open Secret, The: An Introduction to the Theology of Mission   105

Noah   *51, 88*

P

Paul (apostle)   *5, 45, 48, 50, 105, 107*

Pei, Adrian
   The Minority Experience: Navigating Emotional and Organizational Realities   123

Peter (apostle)   *103, 106, 111*

R

Rebellion   *44–46, 49–51, 56, 65, 83*

Redeemer   *90*

Redemption   *44–46, 51–54, 56, 65, 71, 82*

Richardson, Michael   *12*
   Amazing Faith: The Authorized Biography of Bill Bright   4

Rieff, Philip
   My Life Among the Deathworks   27

Riley, William B.   *11*

Runn, Gary
   "Scattering Gospel Seeds: Moments and Conversations"   *72*

S

salvation   *1, 20–21, 28, 52, 80, 91–92, 93, 96, 98*

Satan   *51, 86*

Scale of Belief   *30–32*

Scripture   *10, 19, 31–32, 32, 39, 42–46, 49–51, 55–56, 60, 79–80, 85, 97, 111, 114, 121–22*

secularism   *17, 25–28, 38, 55–56, 59, 61, 63, 65, 96, 121*

Sellers, Steve   *29*

seven personas   *30*

sin   *6, 10, 17–18, 28, 50–52, 63, 100*

Smith, Wilbur   *13*

Smith, James K. A.
   How (Not) to Be Secular: Reading Charles Taylor   121

Soerens, Matthew
   Inalienable: How Marginalized Kingdom Voices Can Help Save the American Church   123

Son (of God)   *6, 42, 44, 48–49, 81–83, 86, 98, 100, 102–3*

Steiger International   *79, 91, 112*

Stetzer, Ed   *36*

Sustainer, God the   *84, 90*

T

Taylor, Charles   *24–27, 57, 63, 65*
  A Secular Age   *121*

Thomas, Heath
  Gospel of Our King   *47–48*

three core longings   *79, 104, 114*
  peace   *67–69*
  prosperity   *67–69*
  purpose   *67–69*

three-statement stories   *71–73,
  114*

Trinity   *81–82, 98, 107, 114*

Trotman, Dawson   *5*

True Story   *41, 43, 45, 46, 50,
  54, 56–60, 64, 67, 71, 74, 79,
  80, 84–85, 87–88, 90–91, 97,
  100, 105, 111–14, 113–15,
  117, 119*

V

Van Gelder, Craig
  *Participating in God's Mission:
    A Theological Missiology
    for the Church in
    America*   *120*

Vanosky, Paige
  *Thirty-Minute Bible, The: God's
    Story for Everyone*   *66,
    113*

W

White, James Emery

  *Meet Generation Z:
    Understanding and
    Reaching the New Post-
    Christian World*   *36*

Williams, Jarvis J.
  *Redemptive Kingdom Diversity:
    A Biblical Theology of the
    People of God*   *120*

Wright, Brooke
  *Understanding Faith and
    Purpose in the City*   *31*

Wright, Christopher J. H.
  *Mission of God, The: Unlocking
    the Bible's Grand
    Narrative*   *121*

Wright, N. T.
  *New Testament and the People of
    God, The*   *90*

Y

Yang, Daniel
  *Inalienable: How Marginalized
    Kingdom Voices Can
    Help Save the American
    Church*   *123*

Z

Zachary, Vonette   *6*

Zscheile, Dwight J.
  *Participating in God's Mission: A
    Theological Missiology for
    the Church in America*   *7,
    14, 120*

Scripture Index

Genesis
1–3 *84, 113*
1:25 *47*
1:26 *47, 66*
1:26–31 *47*
1:27 *66*
1:28 *47, 88*
2:8–9 *47*
2:17 *50, 51*
2:21–24 *47*
3:1–13 *50*
3:15 *51*
3:22–4:16 *50*
6:1–8:19 *51*
8:17 *88*
8:18–19 *51*
8:21 *51, 88*
9:1 *51, 88*
9:7 *88*
9:12 *88*
10–11 *88*
11:1–8 *50*
12 *88*
12:1–3 *47, 89*
12:2 *51*
17 *88*
17:15–21 *85*
21:1–3 *51*
21:1–7 *85*

22:1–19 *52*

Exodus
1:7 *89*
3:7–12 *47*
19 *89*
19:1–6 *52*
19:3–6 *89*
20–39 *52*
24 *89*

Numbers
14:21 *84*

Deuteronomy
4:36–39 *84*
18:15–18 *52*

Ruth
1:6–18 *48*

1 Samuel
8:5 *52*
10:1 *52*
16:12–13 *52*

2 Samuel
7:4–17 *52*
7:5–17 *48*
7:8–16 *90*

1 Chronicles
17:11–15 *90*

Job

38–42 *49*

Psalms

6–9 *49*

8 *47*

14:2–3 *50, 51*

33 *49*

45 *49*

45:5–7 *84*

47:5–7 *49*

53:1–3 *50, 51*

89:1–10 *49*

89:1–11 *49*

90 *84*

95 *84*

95:1–7 *49*

95:3–7 *85*

103:19 *84*

104 *49*

132:11–18 *90*

139 *113*

139:13–16 *48*

143:2 *50, 51*

Isaiah

9:7 *90*

11:1–3 *90*

14 *50*

42:1–9 *52, 83*

42:6 *52*

49 *52*

49:1–6 *83*

49:6 *52*

49:13 *49*

50 *52*

50:2–9 *83*

51:4 *52*

52:13–53:12 *52, 83*

54:8–9 *52*

59:7–9 *50, 51*

59:12 *50, 51*

61 *52*

65:17–25 *54*

Jeremiah

17:9 *50*

31:35–37 *84*

32:38–39 *87*

32:38–40 *87*

Ezekiel

36:26 *54*

Daniel

7:13–14 *86*

Habakkuk

2:14 *45, 84, 87*

Matthew

4:13–17 *86*

5:1–12 *55*

20:28 *53*

28:18 *82*

28:18–20 *6, 91*

Luke

1:26–55 *52*

6:17–26 *55*

22:20 *55*

John

1:1–4 *82*

1:14 *82*

1:14–18 *82*

2:1–12 *49*

4:46–54 *49*

5:1–17 *49*

6:1–21 *49*

6:44 *42, 69, 94, 102*

9:1–12 *49*

10:7–18 *53*

10:10 *53*

11:17–44 *49*

12:23–24 *53*

12:31–33 *53*

13:1 *53*

13:34 *55*

13:34–35 *107*

14:1–3 *53*

14:15–17 *100*

14:15–31 *53*

14:24–25 *81*

14:25–30 *100*

14:25–31 *53*

15:5–7 *100*

15:18–25 *53*

16:1–10 *100*

16:5–11 *53*

16:12–13 *81*

16:33 *53*

17:25–26 *81*

20:22 *53*

Acts

1:6–8 *103*

1:7–8 *53*

1:8 *53*

2 *103*

2:29–36 *90*

2:42–46 *54*

4:32–37 *55*

10 *111*

10:9–16 *111*

10–11 *103*

10:14 *111*

10:28–29 *111*

10:44 *111*

13:26–36 *90*

15 *54*

15:1–21 *103*

15:8–9 *103*

15:10–11 *103*

15:19–21 *103*

15:20 *103*

18–20 *54*

Romans

1:1–7 *82*

1–3 *51*

1:4 *83*

1:18–3:20 *53*

3:23 *50*

4:1–4 *52*

4–8 *53*

4:18–19 *85*

4:19   *51*
5:1–7   *82*
5:3–5   *108*
5:12–20   *54*
6:1–4   *55*
6:1–14   *107*
8:1–7   *100*
8:1–11   *53, 107*
8:9–11   *55, 100*
8:11–13   *83*
8:18–21   *49*
8:18–25   *49, 54*
8:18–30   *82*
8:20–21   *50*
8:26–30   *100*

1 Corinthians
2   *107*
2:6–16   *100*
2:10   *102*
3:16–17   *100*
12:1–11   *100*
15:3–5   *54*
15:12–23   *54*
15:42–49   *55*

2 Corinthians
3:12–18   *100*
4:5–6   *87*
4:6   *45, 84*
4:7   *107*
4:10   *107*
5:16–17   *55*
6:14–18   *100*

6:16–18   *55*
8:9   *55*

Galatians
1:1–5   *51*
3:6–9   *52*
5:16–25   *100*
6:15   *55*

Ephesians
1–3   *54*
1:11–14   *53*
1:15–19   *102*
1:15–22   *100*
2:1–10   *51*
2:4–10   *55*
2:10   *48, 100*
3:14–21   *53*
4:17–32   *55, 100*
5:15–21   *100*

Philippians
1:15–30   *107*
2:1–8   *106*
2:1–12   *55*
2:5–8   *108*
2:5–11   *107*
3:7–11   *107*

Colossians
1:15   *54*
1:15–20   *54, 84*
1:15–22   *82*
1:15–23   *53*
1:18   *54*

2:8–15   *51*
3–4   *55*
3:9–10   *55*

1 Thessalonians
1:1–2   *54*

1 Timothy
3   *54*
5:1–16   *54*
5:17–25   *54*

Hebrews
1:1–3   *87*
1:1–4   *82*
2:14–18   *83*
4:12   *101*
4:14–16   *52*
6:12–20   *55*
8:8–12   *87*
9–10   *53*
9–11   *52*
9:11–15   *52*
10:19–22   *54*
12:26–27   *54*

James
1:27   *54*
5:7–11   *107*

1 Peter
1:1–5   *55*

1–2   *54*
1:3–11   *107*
1:13–21   *53*
1:17–20   *53*
2:4–10   *87*
2:9–24   *55*
2:11–25   *107*
2:21–24   *106*
3:8–15   *55*
3:18   *83*
4:1–5:11   *55*

2 Peter
1:3–4   *53*
1:3–8   *100*
3:4–13   *54*
3:8–9   *93*
3:9   *94, 95*

1 John
1:7–9   *55*

Revelation
5:9–10   *87*
19:11–18   *82*
19–21   *87*
20–21   *53, 54*
21:1–4   *54*
21:1–8   *82*
21–22   *54*